Speculative Whiteness

Forerunners: Ideas First

Short books of thought-in-process scholarship, where intense
analysis, questioning, and speculation take the lead

FROM THE UNIVERSITY OF MINNESOTA PRESS

After Oil Collective; Ayesha Vemuri and Darin Barney, Editors
Solarities: Seeking Energy Justice

Arnaud Gerspacher
The Owls Are Not What They Seem: Artist as Ethologist

Tyson E. Lewis and Peter B. Hyland
Studious Drift: Movements and Protocols for a Postdigital Education

Mick Smith and Jason Young
Does the Earth Care? Indifference, Providence, and Provisional Ecology

Caterina Albano
Out of Breath: Vulnerability of Air in Contemporary Art

Gregg Lambert
The World Is Gone: Philosophy in Light of the Pandemic

Grant Farred
Only a Black Athlete Can Save Us Now

Anna Watkins Fisher
Safety Orange

Heather Warren-Crow and Andrea Jonsson
Young-Girls in Echoland: #Theorizing Tiqqun

Joshua Schuster and Derek Woods
Calamity Theory: Three Critiques of Existential Risk

Daniel Bertrand Monk and Andrew Herscher
The Global Shelter Imaginary: IKEA Humanitarianism and Rightless Relief

Catherine Liu
Virtue Hoarders: The Case against the Professional Managerial Class

Christopher Schaberg
Grounded: Perpetual Flight . . . and Then the Pandemic

Marquis Bey
The Problem of the Negro as a Problem for Gender

Cristina Beltrán
Cruelty as Citizenship: How Migrant Suffering Sustains White Democracy

Hil Malatino
Trans Care

Sarah Juliet Lauro
Kill the Overseer! The Gamification of Slave Resistance

Alexis L. Boylan, Anna Mae Duane, Michael Gill, and Barbara Gurr
Furious Feminisms: Alternate Routes on *Mad Max: Fury Road*

(Continued on page 108)

Speculative Whiteness
Science Fiction and the Alt-Right

Jordan S. Carroll

University of Minnesota Press

MINNEAPOLIS
LONDON

ISBN 978-1-5179-1708-1 (PB)
ISBN 978-1-4529-7088-2 (Ebook)
ISBN 978-1-4529-7255-8 (Manifold)

Published by the University of Minnesota Press, 2024
111 Third Avenue South, Suite 290
Minneapolis, MN 55401-2520
www.upress.umn.edu

Available as a Manifold edition at manifold.umn.edu

The University of Minnesota is an equal-opportunity educator
and employer.

Contents

Introduction: Fascist Worldmaking

THE FIRST MAJOR NEO-NAZI PARTY in the United States was led by a science fiction fan, James H. Madole.[1] Like many science fiction fans, he spent his isolated teenage years dabbling in chemistry and astronomy experiments, looking up to scientists as an elite who'd someday remake society. But instead of embracing technocracy, Madole turned to fascism. He found a ready mentor in Charles B. Hudson, a science fiction author who published a pro-Nazi bulletin that earned him a sedition indictment during the Second World War. Soon after the Axis powers were defeated, Madole attempted to organize right-wing science fiction fans into the totalitarian Animist Party, which was announced in the Spring 1946 issue of *Startling Stories*.[2] Although this group did not last, Madole's fascist connections brought him to the attention of the National Renaissance Party in 1949, and he quickly rose to the top of the newly established

1. Nicholas Goodrick-Clarke, *Black Sun: Aryan Cults, Esoteric Nazism, and the Politics of Identity* (New York: New York University Press, 2002), 72–87. See also Kevin Coogan, *Dreamer of the Day: Francis Parker Yockey and the Postwar Fascist International* (Brooklyn, N.Y.: Autonomedia, 1999), 418–20, 524.

2. Coogan, *Dreamer*, 419; "Animalist [sic] Party," *Fancyclopedia* 3, July 6, 2022, https://fancyclopedia.org/Animalist_Party; James H. Madole, "New Party for Animals or Something," *Startling Stories* 13, no. 3 (Spring 1946), 106, https://archive.org/details/StartlingStoriesV13N031946Spring/page /n105/mode/2up.

organization. Madole led the NRP for the next thirty years, often provoking street brawls between his uniformed stormtroopers and the counterdemonstrators who protested his rallies.

Adolf Hitler stood at the center of NRP's dogma, but Madole also drew upon occult ideas as well as science fiction influences. Madole believed that once Jews and people of color had been eliminated, America would be transformed into a New Atlantis that would rival the lost continent that he considered the Aryans' high-tech homeland. Madole predicted that Atlantean eugenicists would breed a new species of "God-like human mutations" who would rule over "Mass Man" before eventually culling him from the gene pool.[3] Using a term coined by science fiction author Olaf Stapledon, he calls these Aryan mutants "Homo Superior," the next stage in evolution.[4] Compared to these demigods, humans from the twentieth century would look like "mental and physical anachronisms."[5] Once fascism prevailed on earth, the Aryan race would head out to start an interplanetary empire: "The ultimate destiny of man lies in the stars."[6] As we shall see, Madole's vision is a racially explicit version of a narrative found throughout science fiction fan culture, whose members often saw themselves as the earliest ancestors of a new hyperintelligent species destined for space.

3. James H. Madole, "'The New Atlantis': A Blueprint for an Aryan 'Garden of Eden' in North America (Part IX)," in Kerry Bolton, *Phoenix Rising: The Epic Saga of James H. Madole* (Paraparaumu Beach, New Zealand: Renaissance Press, 2001), 37. This publication was consulted in the Stephen O. Murray and Keelung Hong Special Collections, Michigan State University Libraries.

4. James H. Madole, "'The New Atlantis': A Blueprint for an Aryan 'Garden of Eden' in North America (Part II)," in Kerry Bolton, *Phoenix Rising: The Epic Saga of James H. Madole* (Paraparaumu Beach, New Zealand: Renaissance Press, 2001), Stephen O. Murray and Keelung Hong Special Collections, Michigan State University Libraries, 16.

5. James H. Madole, qtd in Jeffrey Kaplan and Leonard Weinberg, *The Emergence of a Euro-American Radical Right* (New Brunswick, N.J.: Rutgers University Press, 1998), 114.

6. James H. Madole qtd in Coogan, *Dreamer*, 418.

Although revered by occult fascists, Madole has mostly been forgotten. An off-putting figure who appeared at actions wearing a tightly buttoned suit jacket, a pair of thick glasses, and a crash helmet, Madole did not stand a chance against a rising generation of fascist leaders such as George Lincoln Rockwell, the charismatic founder of the American Nazi Party.[7] Nevertheless, the Madole case shows that fascism made deep connections with fandom.

White nationalism and science fiction remain intertwined to this day. Public perception equates the alt-right with geek culture. GOP strategist Rick Wilson characterized the movement's adherents as "mostly childless single men who masturbate to anime."[8] Some self-described otaku pushed back, dissociating themselves from the alt-right.[9] However, many of the alt-right's leaders confirm the nerdiness of contemporary white nationalism. Although Richard Spencer models his public image after clean-cut fascists like Rockwell or David Duke, during his more unguarded conversations he brags about owning a light saber, obsesses over Christopher Nolan, and discusses every development in the *Dune* franchise with avid interest.[10]

Matthew Heimbach lacks Spencer's polish and prominence, but as cofounder of the Traditionalist Worker Party he played an important role in bringing together neo-Nazis, Klansmen, neo-

7. Goodrick-Clarke, *Black Sun,* 72.

8. Rick Wilson (@TheRickWilson), "Actual quote, not that it will matter: 'The screamers on AltRight who love Trump are mostly childless single men who masturbate to anime,'" Twitter, January 19, 2016, 5:32 p.m., https://twitter.com/therickwilson/status/689621554636984320?lang=en.

9. Lynzee Loveridge, "Otaku on the Receiving End of GOP Strategist's Trump Supporter Insult," *Anime News Network*, January 20, 2016, https://www.animenewsnetwork.com/interest/2016-01-20/otaku-on-the-receiving-end-of-gop-strategist-trump-supporter-insult/.97755.

10. Jordan S. Carroll, "Race Consciousness: Fascism and Frank Herbert's 'Dune,'" *Los Angeles Review of Books,* November 19, 2020, https://lareviewofbooks.org/article/race-consciousness-fascism-and-frank-herberts-dune/.

Confederates, and skinheads in a brief but dangerous alliance.[11] According to Heimbach, his entrée into white nationalism began with the British science fiction wargame *Warhammer 40,000*. The game depicts the eternal struggles of fanatical Space Marines as they kill mutants, aliens, and heretics in the name of their dictatorial ruler, the God-Emperor of Mankind. It's a male fantasy Klaus Theweleit would have recognized as conducive to fascism: cold and unfeeling soldiers armored in impenetrable metal devote their lives to eradicating an endless flood of formless, feminized creatures embodying chaotic emotions.[12] Some Space Marines even deck themselves out in iron crosses and death's-head insignia. But the original creators at Games Workshop intended *Warhammer 40,000* as a parody of authoritarian violence *à la* British comic magazine *2000 AD*'s Judge Dredd, and the company disavows the hobby's small fascist fan base. Many players have fought back against the fascists, reaffirming the game as a critique of fascism.[13]

Heimbach argues that *Warhammer 40,000* helped him see that classical liberal ideals fail to apply in the struggle against inhuman enemies.[14] He describes himself as waging a comparable battle against a "Satanic culture" that must be prosecuted with the

11. Vegas Tenold, *Everything You Love Will Burn: Inside the Rebirth of White Nationalism in America* (New York: Nation Books, 2018).

12. Klaus Theweleit, *Male Fantasies, Vol. 1: Women, Floods, Bodies, History,* trans. Stephen Conway, Erica Carter, and Chris Turner (Minneapolis: University of Minnesota Press, 1987). See Jordan S. Carroll, "The Politics of 'Space Marine,'" *The California Aggie,* November 17, 2011, https://theaggie.org/2011/11/17/column-the-politics-of-%E2%80%9Cspace -marine%E2%80%9D/.

13. Jordan S. Carroll, "Welcome to Warhammer 40k's Anti-fascist Future," *Polygon,* October 25, 2022, https://www.polygon.com/23414657 /warhammer-40k-anti-fascism-space-marines-capitalism-leagues-of -votann-hate.

14. Matthew Heimbach, "Science Fiction Fascism Part II: Warhammer 40k," *Trad Worker,* February 7, 2014, https://web.archive.org/web /20170916001748/https://www.tradworker.org/2014/02/science-fiction -fascism-part-ii-warhammer-40k/.

same unyielding zeal as the Space Marines' crusade against demons from another dimension.[15] Alt-right meme makers later transformed Donald Trump's campaign staff into characters from the *Warhammer 40,000* universe, with the future president appearing as the God-Emperor himself.[16] Heimbach invoked similar fantasies while stumping for a grand fascist alliance, driving a beater he named *Serenity* after the spaceship in Joss Whedon's *Firefly* series.[17]

Science fiction thinking turns out to be surprisingly prevalent in the alt-right and antecedent white nationalist movements.[18] Fascists often speculate about zombies, supermen, and space explorers while envisioning the founding of a Cosmic Reich. However, this book will show that science fiction serves as more than just a pop culture reference in fascist discourse. While the field of science fiction studies has long argued that speculative genres help promote radical change, the alt-right has interpreted science fiction to say that a fascist world is possible.[19]

Metapolitics

White supremacist movements have long weaponized popular culture. The second Ku Klux Klan wave started as a fan response to D. W. Griffith's *The Birth of a Nation* (1915), and the Klan propagated itself throughout the 1920s with books, music, plays, and even a baseball team.[20] Many theorists have examined how German Nazis and Italian fascists aestheticized violence while presenting their

15. Heimbach.

16. "God-Emperor Trump," *Know Your Meme,* accessed July 6, 2022, https://knowyourmeme.com/memes/god-emperor-trump.

17. Tenold, *Everything You Love,* 39, 195.

18. See Brooks Landon, *Science Fiction after 1900: From the Steam Man to the Stars* (New York: Routledge, 2002), 4–10.

19. See, for example, Darko Suvin, "On the Poetics of the Science Fiction Genre," *College English* 34, no. 3 (December 1972): 372–81.

20. Felix Harcourt, *Ku Klux Kulture: America and the Klan in the 1920s* (Chicago: University of Chicago Press, 2017), 182.

order as a monumental spectacle.[21] Hitler's fulminations against an allegedly Jewish-controlled culture industry inspired Rockwell and his successors in the White Power movement to critique mass media for promoting what they saw as racial degeneracy, something they hoped to counteract with an alternative culture extolling white purity's virtues.[22] White Power activists have pursued this project through Nazi-themed punk, metal, and folk acts, as well as through online forums where they debate interpretations of popular media.[23]

The alt-right believes that, as Andrew Breitbart put it, "politics is downstream from culture."[24] Alt-right figures such as Spencer borrowed the concept of "metapolitics" from the reactionary Gramscians of the French New Right.[25] Through metapolitics, they hope to undermine liberal hegemony by using cultural counter-messaging to promote white identitarianism's pre-political assumptions. Policy changes will follow, they claim, once they have cultivated fascist attitudes in white people through right-wing media manipulation.

These ideas reflect the influence of British fascist Jonathan Bowden, who believed that mass-cultural forms such as science

21. Lutz P. Koepnick, "Fascist Aesthetics Revisited," *Modernism/modernity* 6, no. 1 (January 1999): 51–73.

22. C. Richard King and David J. Leonard, *Beyond Hate: White Power and Popular Culture* (Burlington Vt.: Ashgate 2014), 2–5.

23. Kirsten Dyck, *Reichsrock: The International Web of White-Power and Neo-Nazi Hate Music* (New Brunswick, N.J.: Rutgers University Press, 2017). King and Leonard, *Beyond Hate,* 7–8.

24. To avoid directing internet traffic and advertising revenue to active far-right websites, all citations referencing them direct readers to copies kept by the Internet Archive's Wayback Machine instead of the original URLs. Andrew Breitbart qtd in Thaddeus G. McCotter, "Pop Cultural Conservatism, Year One A.B. (After Breitbart)," *Breitbart.com,* March 1, 2013, https://web.archive.org/web/20240328160627/https://www.breitbart.com/the-media/2013/03/01/pop-cultural-conservatism-year-one-a-b-after-breitbart/.

25. Alexandra Minna Stern, *Proud Boys and the White Ethnostate: How the Alt-Right Is Warping the American Imagination* (Boston: Beacon Press, 2019), 21–32.

fiction novels, fantasy epics, and superhero comics contain subtexts that subvert egalitarianism's official dogma. In a speech republished as "Pulp Fascism," Bowden argues that the protagonist in popular narratives is often a Schmittian sovereign who uses his exceptional power to smash his subhuman foes.[26] Bowden even draws inspiration from Norman Spinrad's *The Iron Dream* (1972), a metafictional narrative that imagines the novel Adolf Hitler would have published if he had become a science fiction novelist after emigrating to the United States in 1919. Anticipating the far-right themes explored in this book, Spinrad's novel ends with a "Master Race" of "superhuman" clones blasting off into space to colonize other planets after all Earth's genetically inferior populations have been exterminated.[27] Spinrad intended the novel's over-the-top genocidal themes as an attack on the racism and militarism implicit in many science fiction classics, but the author was disturbed to discover the book was recommended by the American Nazi Party.[28] Bowden joins a long line of fascists who find value in Spinrad's hyperbolic sendup of their creed. As Bowden suggests, "fantasy enables certain people to have an irony bypass."[29] Using these strategies, the alt-right reclaims for itself the reactionary figures satirized or villainized in speculative genres. In other words, fascists figured out the subversion and containment model, i.e., the critical notion that orthodoxy must reproduce heretical ideas even if only to negate them.[30]

26. Jonathan Bowden, "Pulp Fascism," *Counter-Currents*, March 25, 2013, https://web.archive.org/web/20230202080529/https://counter-currents.com/2013/03/pulp-fascism/. See also Jonathan Bowden, *Pulp Fascism: Right-Wing Themes in Comics, Graphic Novels, and Popular Literature* (San Francisco: Counter-Currents, 2013).

27. Norman Spinrad, *The Iron Dream* (New York: Avon, 1972), 241.

28. Norman Spinrad, "Psychopolitics and Science Fiction," *Science Fiction in the Real World* (Carbondale and Edwardsville: Southern Illinois University Press, 1990), 158.

29. Bowden, "Pulp Fascism," n.p.

30. Stephen Greenblatt, *Shakespearean Negotiations: The Circulation of Social Energy in Renaissance England* (Berkeley: University of California Press, 1988), 30–36.

The alt-right must be understood as an interpretive project as well as a political movement. Science fiction, as Samuel R. Delany tells us, takes place in the subjunctive, detailing "events that have not happened."[31] For example, this includes "predictive tales" covering "events that might happen" and "cautionary dystopias" featuring "events that have not happened yet."[32] Building on this argument, Steven Shaviro shows that science fiction sets up "thought experiments" that need never happen but nevertheless tell us about what could happen.[33] We might go even further to suggest that science fiction often leaves us uncertain about how we should interpret the relationship between the possible future and the actual present. A science fiction narrative might be read simultaneously as blueprint, warning, forecast, wish-dream, and counterfactual. Our critical understanding of science fiction relies on what might be called speculative indeterminacy, the unresolvable tensions between multiple forms of futurity.

The alt-right, however, reads science fiction as an imperative, dictating events that must happen or must not happen. As such, the central interpretive problem for the alt-right is whether a work of science fiction promotes Aryan interests by commanding white audiences to preserve and improve the race. Fascists thereby strip science fiction of its speculative indeterminacy. While most science fiction critics interpret the genre as experimenting freely with manifold new possibilities, the alt-right believes that science fiction compels white people to realize the inner potential already endowed to them by biological and cultural evolution.

Science fiction's attempts at autocritique prove uniquely vulnerable to this approach. Science fiction creators including not only

    31. Samuel R. Delany, "About 5,750 Words," *The Jewel-Hinged Jaw: Notes on the Language of Science Fiction* (Middletown, Conn.: Wesleyan University Press, 2009), 11.
    32. Delany, 11.
    33. Steven Shaviro, "(ENG) Steven Shaviro: Extrapolation, Speculation, Fabulation," *YouTube,* October 18, 2021, https://youtu.be /mbu4hBe2GA4.

Spinrad but also Frank Herbert, Alan Moore, and Paul Verhoeven have often summoned the specter of fascism only to exorcise it. These narratives invite audiences to take pleasure in reactionary power fantasies drawn from the genre's history before revealing to them that they have inadvertently joined the devil's party. Alt-right reading protocols foreshorten this critique, highlighting the text's invocation of fascist enjoyment while omitting the moment of critical estrangement that would banish those authoritarian possibilities. They see the dystopia as a political program.

But I want to argue that speculation serves a more fundamental purpose for the alt-right. The alt-right understands metapolitics as a form of speculative worldmaking that allows them to decide not only which worlds are conceivable but also who has the power to imagine other worlds in the first place. Greg Johnson, editor-in-chief at the alt-right publisher Counter-Currents, suggests that politics is the "art of the possible," but metapolitics changes "people's view of possibility" by altering their "basic ideas about how the world works and about who they are."[34] Spencer, quoting the same folk definition of politics, reaffirms Johnson's point by saying that "the art of the impossible is exactly the reason our movement should exist."[35] This is why the alt-right is drawn to speculative genres. Metapolitics seeks to transform white nationalism from an unthinkable possibility to an inevitable future.

Jason Reza Jorjani, who cofounded the AltRight Corporation with Spencer and Arktos publisher Daniel Friberg, developed this notion further in his reflections on authority. Jorjani argues that a small elite of "authors" possess the ability to reshape "the 'worldhood' of our world at the most fundamental level, namely the level

34. Greg Johnson, qtd in Thomas J. Main, *The Rise of the Alt-Right* (Washington, D.C.: Brookings Institution Press, 2018), 12.

35. Richard Spencer, qtd in Kevin Musgrave and Jeff Tischauser, "Radical Traditionalism, Metapolitics, and Identitarianism: The Rhetoric of Richard Spencer," *boundary2*, September 1, 2019, https://www.boundary2 .org/2019/09/kevin-musgrave-and-jeff-tischauser-radical-traditionalism -metapolitics-and-identitarianism-the-rhetoric-of-richard-spencer/.

of the folklore that conditions the substratum of the collective and personal unconscious."[36] Unlike the mainstream politicians and influencers who merely pretend to have power, authors have phenomenal "authority to define the limits of [their] world, or at least to play a significant role in defining those parameters that determine what is or is not 'possible.'"[37] Jorjani asserts that the masses will never participate in this process of worldmaking because not everyone "deserves a future," and indeed he predicts that most people will be subjugated or exterminated to make way for Nietzschean supermen who will use post-Singularity technologies to rewrite existence as they please.[38] Through metapolitical authorship, the alt-right opens up new potential futures for powerful white people while shutting them down for everything else.

Metapolitics can best be explained through the analytic framework developed by Mark Jerng. He argues that race and genre operate at the level of modal imagination, a faculty that allows people to make prospective predictions about what might happen as well as retrospective judgments about how things could have gone otherwise.[39] Through modal imagination we speculate on what is probable, possible, and impossible, and without it we couldn't conceive of anything that is not present in the immediate moment.[40] Race and genre structure our expectations about the world, interacting with one another in complex ways. Jerng argues that genres manipulate racialized meanings when "establishing situations and justifying actions while making others seem less possible or realizable."[41] At the same time, "race shapes genre" because it "composes expectations for what the world might look like and activates rules for knowing

36. Jason Reza Jorjani, *Uber Man* (London: Arktos, 2022), 68. Kindle.
37. Jorjani, 69.
38. Jorjani, 72, 170.
39. Mark C. Jerng, *Racial Worldmaking: The Power of Popular Fiction* (New York: Fordham University Press, 2018), 13–14.
40. Adrian M. S. Piper, "Impartiality, Compassion, and Modal Imagination," *Ethics* 101, no. 4 (July 1991): 726–57.
41. Jerng, *Racial Worldmaking*, 19.

the world."[42] When the alt-right uses science fiction as a tool to change metapolitics, they intervene in the racialized worldview that constitutes the grounds for determining what is politically or socially possible.

I want to underscore here that I do not simply mean that alt-right adherents use science fictional narratives to paint what they see as attractive pictures of their ethnically cleansed utopias.[43] Although they certainly do that, much more is going on here. My argument is that the alt-right seizes upon speculative genres to dictate who has the right to speculate in the first place.

The alt-right asserts ownership over science fiction because they think white people maintain a monopoly on modal imagination. Nonwhite people, they suggest, dwell in a state of modal impoverishment, cut off from possibility. The alt-right construes nonwhite people as insensitive to the consequences of their own actions and unable to envisage anything other than what already exists. Even more fundamentally, the alt-right asserts that there is nothing more to nonwhite people than what they have already become. According to the fascists, only white people may change, evolve, or open onto new possibilities. The myth of modal impoverishment insinuates that nonwhite people have no place in either the science fiction field or the futures that it conjures. We see the alt-right trying to police the boundaries of science fiction every time they protest when a person of color is cast in a genre film. It is not simply that the alt-right hates diversity in cinema: they're offended by the idea that nonwhite people might exist in other possible worlds. The fact that a renaissance of Afrofuturist and otherwise antiracist science fiction has disproven the alt-right's exclusive claim to the future only makes them more eager to colonize the genre for themselves.

42. Jerng, 19.
43. See Edward K. Chan, "The White Power Utopia and the Reproduction of Victimized Whiteness," in *Race and Utopian Desire in American Literature and Society*, ed. Patricia Ventura and Edward K. Chan, 139–59 (Cham, Switzerland: Palgrave Macmillan, 2019).

Through metapolitical activism, the alt-right strives to redefine the public's fundamental ideas about the world, including its sense of time and temporality. Only white people, we are told, retain the future-oriented capacities and dispositions required to make progress. They argue that whiteness enables men to delay gratification in order to plan and save.[44] Whiteness, they say, is also the force that propels white men to engage in speculative ventures that require foresight, vision, and a tolerance for entrepreneurial risk.[45] We hear that whiteness expands the scope of its members' thoughts and actions, allowing them to operate on a grand scale in both space and time.[46] White blood is touted as the font of innovation, creating every ingenious novelty and invention that built the modern world.[47]

Above all, whiteness appears as an inborn tendency to transcend the indexical present. For the alt-right, whiteness represents a matrix of possibilities more important than any actual accomplishments the white race may have already achieved. Before killing nine Black people at a church in Charleston, Dylann Roof wrote in his journal, "I am not fighting for what White people are, but for what we have the potential to be."[48] Whiteness appears as consubstantial with speculative futurity.

We can therefore understand speculative whiteness as an ideological complex that promotes the following series of mutually reinforcing myths: (1) white people maintain a unique aptitude for innovative speculation, (2) speculative imagination is absent

44. Madison Grant, *The Passing of the Great Race: or, The Racial Basis of European History* (New York: Charles Scribner's Sons, 1919), 170.

45. Jason Reza Jorjani, *Faustian Futurist* (London, Arktos, 2020), 81.

46. Frank Raymond interview with Henrik Palmgren, "The Caucasian Mind: Transcending Biological Needs," *Red Ice Radio*, April 18, 2016, https://web.archive.org/web/20231003034845/https://redice.tv/red-ice-radio/the-caucasian-mind-transcending-biological-needs.

47. Adolf Hitler, *Mein Kampf,* trans. Ralph Manheim (Boston: Mariner, 1999), 288–91.

48. Dylann Roof qtd in Rachel Jane Liebert, *Psycurity: Colonialism, Paranoia, and the War on Imagination* (New York: Routledge, 2018), 22.

or deficient in nonwhite populations, (3) whiteness possesses a speculative value only realizable in a high-tech fascist future, (4) science fiction and other speculative genres are inherently white, and (5) white people become aware of their potential by seeing it manifested in speculative narratives.

Although the alt-right provides a major focal point for this book, my goal is to show that speculative whiteness is a persistent theme in science fiction culture and the broader far-right movement. In the first chapter, I will explore how science fiction culture has often suggested that some people are genetically predisposed toward future-orientation and long-term thinking, a notion that is racialized in libertarian and fascist thought. White elites often appear in right-wing narratives as mutants, aliens, and other futuristic beings who are beset by the backward masses. In the next chapter, I will consider how the alt-right and its forebears equated speculative risk-taking with white masculinity. Drawing on De Witt Douglas Kilgore, I show that white nationalists imagined space exploration as the next step in European settler-colonial Manifest Destiny, allowing white men to steel themselves toward danger while transcending earthly limits.[49] Finally, I offer a brief glance at antifascist science fiction narratives that challenge speculative whiteness. Over the course of this study, I shall show the stories told in the name of speculative whiteness are fundamentally incoherent. Fascist science fictions would have us believe that revolutionary historical changes can emerge from a white racial essence that remains forever ahistorical and invariant.[50] By laying bare these irresolvable inconsistencies in speculative whiteness, this book hopes to help wrest the speculative from those who would limit it to the service of oppression.

49. De Witt Douglas Kilgore, *Afrofuturism: Space, Race, and Visions of Utopia in Space* (Philadelphia: University of Philadelphia Press, 2003), 76, 223.

50. See George L. Mosse, *Toward the Final Solution: A History of European Racism* (New York: Howard Fertig, 1978), 31.

Speculative whiteness has deep roots in racist thought. Whiteness has often reserved for itself "a capacity to know and control the future."[51] One of the earlier examples of speculative whiteness in scientific racism was formulated in 1901 by Edward Ross, an influential nativist and eugenicist who argued that some races have more "foresight" than others.[52] Ross decomposed foresight into two interconnected elements that we will see throughout this study: "a lively imagination of remote experiences to come" and "self-control that can deny present cravings, or resist temptation in favor of the thrifty course recommended by reason."[53] Alleged differences in foresight prompted Ross to divide populations into "the provident races," who are motivated by "ideas," and the "impulsivists," who "remain absorbed in sensations."[54] According to Ross, the disciplined imagination of white people allows them to build a more prosperous economic future while Asian and Indigenous peoples "live from hand to mouth taking no thought of the morrow."[55]

Speculative whiteness is by no means limited to fascist ideologues, but it proved paramount in postwar white nationalism. No slogan is more important to the movement than David Lane's Fourteen Words—"We must secure the existence of our people and a future for White children"—but many other racists have laid claim to the future as well.[56] Spencer provoked outrage by quoting the Hitler Youth's song in *Cabaret*: "tomorrow belongs to us."[57] Johnson's *The*

---

51. Linda Martín Alcoff, *The Future of Whiteness* (Malden, Mass.: Polity, 2015), 24.

52. Edward A. Ross, "The Causes of Race Superiority," *The Annals of the American Academy of Political and Social Science* 18 (July 1901): 76. See also Nell Irvin Painter, *The History of White People* (New York: Norton, 2010), 251–54.

53. Ross, "Race Superiority," 76.

54. Ross, 76.

55. Ross, 75.

56. David Lane qtd in Stern, *Proud Boys and the White Ethnostate*, 53.

57. Richard Spencer, ".@joshtpm No, tomorrow belongs to us," Twitter, March 18, 2017, 5:44 p.m. ET, https://twitter.com/RichardBSpencer /status/843216482838355968.

White Nationalist Manifesto defines his political tendency as "white people who have decided to have a future again." He compares the white response to "demographic decline" with the science fiction scenario in which people who have heard reports of an earthbound asteroid give themselves over to "short-term hedonism," partying like there's no tomorrow.[58] Falling white birthrates, he suggests, mean the end of the future.

The alt-right's ontology commits whiteness to the future even as it confines nonwhite people to the past or present. White nationalist literature posits that Jews follow a mechanical causality whose strict determinism prevents them from making the daring leaps into the future.[59] Muslims supposedly represent a recrudescence of a medieval past.[60] Racists cast Asians as imitators, capable of maintaining white civilization but never creating anything new.[61] Black and Indigenous people allegedly exist outside of historical time.[62] Often we're told that nonwhite populations obey present-oriented appetites, preventing them from ever thinking beyond their immediate circumstances.[63] If whiteness in racist discourse endows European-descended people with the ability to inhabit a wide array of possible futures, its absence consigns other races to a dwindling range of possibilities.[64]

58. Greg Johnson, *The White Nationalist Manifesto* (San Francisco: Counter-Currents, 2018), 6–8.

59. Francis Parker Yockey (Ulrick Varange), *Imperium: The Philosophy of History and Politics* (1948; repr. Sausalito, Calif.: The Noontide Press, 1962), 12–16, 422–39.

60. Daniel Wollenberg, "Defending the West: Cultural Racism and Pan-Europeanism on the Far Right," *Postmedieval: A Journal of Medieval Cultural Studies* 5 (2014): 310.

61. Hitler, *Mein Kampf*, 290–91.

62. Oswald Spengler, *The Decline of the West: Complete in One Volume*, vol. 1 (New York: Knopf, 1937), 167.

63. Richard Lynn, "Racial and Ethnic Differences in Psychopathic Personality," *Personality and Individual Differences* 32 (2002): 294.

64. See Devin Zane Shaw, *Philosophy of Antifascism: Punching Nazis and Fighting White Supremacy* (New York: Roman & Littlefield, 2020), 54.

Fight for the Future

Knowing how often the right yearns for the past, it may seem strange that some reactionaries look to the future. When reactionaries feel a nostalgic desire for lost hierarchies, they tend to call up hazy conceptions of medieval Europe or classical antiquity, which they depict using images drawn from fantasy and related genres.[65] Outside of eschatology, the future appears in many right-wing visions as a decline from these purported golden ages. Glib reactionaries invoke *1984, Brave New World,* or *The Matrix* to emphasize how far they think society has fallen. White nationalists have authored dystopian novels featuring tyrannical governments dedicated to enforcing multiculturalism and political correctness, a dismal subgenre best known for William Pierce's *The Turner Diaries* (1978) that also includes Ward Kendall's *Hold Back This Day* (1999) and William Wilson's *Utopia X* (2004).[66]

But fascists have always been willing to embrace the most revolutionary forms of modernism and modernization so long as they can be made to secure a future that strengthens the powers of the privileged.[67] Italian fascism drew early inspiration and adherents from the Futurist avant-garde, while Nazi Germany worshipped in the cult of the engineer.[68] Even when the fascists were not promis-

65. Louie Dean Valencia-García, ed., *Far-Right Revisionism and the End of History: Alt/Histories* (New York: Routledge, 2020); Kristian A. Bjørkelo, "Elves are Jews with Pointy Ears and Gay Magic: White Nationalist Readings of *The Elder Scrolls V: Skyrim,*" *The International Journal of Computer Research* 20, no. 3 (September 2020), http://gamestudies.org/2003/articles/bjorkelo.

66. Edward K. Chan, *The Racial Horizon of Utopia: Unthinking the Future of Race in Late Twentieth-Century American Utopian Novels* (New York: Peter Lang, 2016), 194–200.

67. Corey Robin, *The Reactionary Mind: Conservatism from Edmund Burke to Donald Trump,* 2nd ed. (New York: Oxford University Press, 2018), 24–28.

68. Simonetta Falasca-Zamponi, "The Artist to Power? Futurism, Fascism, and the Avant-Garde," *Theory, Culture & Society* 12, no. 2 (1996):

ing technoscientific marvels, they claimed to represent what Roger Griffin calls "'a sense of a beginning,' the mood of standing on the threshold of a new world."[69]

Alt-right science fiction may also seem unlikely because we normally think of anti-racist authors such as Octavia Butler or Ursula K. Le Guin when we think of science fiction, but this critical consensus results from a long political struggle within science fiction culture. As andré m. carrington shows in *Speculative Blackness: The Future of Race in Science Fiction*, science fiction was widely presumed white for much of its history. The science fiction field, he observes, was characterized by "both the overrepresentation of White people among the ranks of SF authors and the overrepresentation of White people's experiences within SF texts."[70] During recent controversies such as Racefail 09, science fiction writers critiqued the field's racism.[71] But, as Isiah Lavender III notes, despite a flurry of antiracist academic conferences and BIPOC-authored anthologies, the white problem persists in science fiction fandom and scholarly culture.[72] Others have detailed white supremacy's hold on other speculative genres such as fantasy, as well.[73]

These liberatory movements in the field have coincided with a deep, right-wing tendency in the genre. As David Forbes has ar-

---

39–58; Jeffrey Herf, *Reactionary Modernism: Technology, Culture, and Politics in Weimar and the Third Reich* (Cambridge: Cambridge University Press, 1984).

69. Roger Griffin, *Modernism and Fascism: The Sense of a Beginning under Mussolini and Hitler* (New York: Palgrave, 2007), 1.

70. andré m. carrington, *Speculative Blackness: The Future of Race in Science Fiction* (Minneapolis: University of Minnesota Press, 2016), 16

71. See, for example, Nalo Hopkinson, "Report from Planet Midnight," *Report from Planet Midnight* (Oakland, Calif.: PM Press, 2012), 27–50.

72. Isiah Lavender III, "Science Fiction and Racism: Decolonizing the White Problem, an Essay in Three Parts," *Foundation* 50, no. 139 (2021): 106–20.

73. Ebony Elizabeth Thomas, *The Dark Fantastic: Race and Imagination from Harry Potter to the Hunger Games* (New York: New York University Press, 2019), 4–7.

gued, science fiction's family tree includes a line of reactionary science fiction running from Robert A. Heinlein, Larry Niven, and Jerry Pournelle to the latest Baen military science fiction paperback.[74] Even science fiction's contemporary canon sometimes lends itself to this trend. David M. Higgins demonstrates that science fiction informed the alt-right's sense of victimhood by presenting "reverse colonization" narratives in which imperial powers oppress white men.[75]

Throughout these speculative imaginings, though, the alt-right maintains a complicated relationship with science fiction culture. Some critics who follow Darko Suvin in defining science fiction as progressive treat the genre's reactionary elements as inessential holdovers from the pulp tradition.[76] Aaron Santesso is one of the few scholars advocating for the opposing position. He argues that science fiction is plagued by fascist tropes—e.g., militaristic supermen saving futuristic utopias from biologically inferior invaders—that continually reassert themselves as right-wing in otherwise apparently progressive texts.[77] This work is very useful, but it's worth stressing that even reactionary narrative conventions can be resignified to take on other political valences. Furthermore, we should emphasize along with Santesso science fiction's ideological "diversity."[78] Its history contains both Madole and the fans who met his Animist Party proposal with skepticism. Science fiction fandom has always been fractious. *Astounding Science Fiction* editor John W. Campbell, Jr., may have dominated early science fiction while promoting notoriously right-wing views, but the field also included

74. David Forbes, *The Old Iron Dream* (Oakland, Calif.: Inkshares, 2014).

75. David M. Higgins, *Reverse Colonization: Science Fiction, Imperial Fantasy, and Alt-Victimhood* (Iowa City: University of Iowa Press, 2021), 1–3.

76. Aaron Santesso, "Fascism and Science Fiction," *Science Fiction Studies* 41 (2014): 138–39.

77. Santesso, 147–48.

78. Santesso, 156.

countervailing influences such as the Futurians, a circle of science fiction authors with communist connections.[79]

However, before we absolve science fiction, we should remember that, even among the Futurians, James Blish liked to provoke Trotskyist Judith Merril by claiming to be a "book fascist" sympathetic to fascism in theory if not practice.[80] Science fiction has never been innocent of fascism. I do not want to cede science fiction to the white nationalists, but I also do not want to downplay science fiction culture's complicity by treating right-wing extremists as mere interlopers who arrived late to pervert the genre by imposing their own agenda on it.

But if we reject genre essentialism, we still need to explain why some genres lend themselves to fascist appropriations while others do not. National Socialist Black Metal quickly became a cottage industry, but white power rap remains a novelty. Each genre is a terrain of struggle, shaped and reshaped through political interventions, but not all battlefields offer every side the same strategic advantages. Riven by political contradictions, science fiction includes racist, sexist, and elitist formations as well as critical and egalitarian ones. The alt-right did not project speculative whiteness onto science fiction: it pieced it together out of components already found within the genre.

This reconfirms Stuart Hall's argument that the radical right does not invent itself out of whole cloth: it "takes the elements which are already constructed into place, dismantles them, reconstitutes them into a new logic, and articulates the space in a new way, polarizing it

79. Alec Nevala-Lee, *Astounding: John W. Campbell, Isaac Asimov, Robert A. Heinlein, L. Ron Hubbard, and the Golden Age of Science Fiction* (New York: Dey St., 2018), 122–23, 360–69; Sam Moskowitz, *The Immortal Storm: A History of Science Fiction Fandom* (Westport, Conn.: Hyperion Press, 1954); Damon Knight, *The Futurians: The Story of the Science Fiction "Family" of the 30's That Produced Today's Top SF Writers and Editors* (New York: John Day, 1977).

80. Knight, *The Futurians*, 155.

to the right."[81] Here the alt-right did more than simply affirm the reactionary aspects of science fiction while negating its emancipatory
dimensions. Even among commentators on the alt-right, this kind
of selective interpretation comes off as crude and unconvincing.[82]
Instead, the alt-right has imaginatively reconfigured science fiction
by positioning the genre's reactionary impulse as the motive force
driving its progressive elements forward. They believe that white
supremacy is the source of science fiction's utopian aspirations.

White supremacist Frank Raymond provides the most systematic
articulation of this idea in his science fiction novel *Sweet Dreams
and Terror Cells*. Raymond argues that people of color are ham-
pered by what he calls the "energy conservation constraint," an
innate tendency to be satisfied once immediate biological needs are
met.[83] According to Raymond, this leaves people of color with no
inclination to spend time on imaginative play or technoscientific
innovation. Raymond contrasts this racialized condition with the
Caucasian mind that stretches "out into the unknown, breaking free
from the hard ground of the here-and-now practicality and harsh
reality of the concrete of the street and the demands of the belly."[84]
Raymond likes to quote Goethe's *Faust* to describe this aspect of
the white spirit: "at what is vast and mystical we thrill."[85] This is
a mind that explores not only reality but also possible worlds in

81. Stuart Hall, "The Great Moving Right Show," in *The Hard Road to
Renewal: Thatcherism and the Crisis of the Left* (London: Verso, 1988), 44.

82. James J. O'Meara, "Lennart Svensson's *Science Fiction Seen from
the Right*," *Counter-Currents,* November 23, 2016, https://web.archive.org
/web/20230604010229/https://counter-currents.com/2016/11/science
-fiction-seen-from-the-right/.

83. Frank Raymond interview with Henrik Palmgren, "The Caucasian
Mind: Transcending Biological Needs," *Red Ice Radio,* April 18, 2016, https://
web.archive.org/web/20231003034845/https://redice.tv/red-ice-radio/the
-caucasian-mind-transcending-biological-needs.

84. Frank Raymond, *Sweet Dreams and Terror Cells,* vol. 1: *When
Giants Break the Spell,* 2nd ed. (n.p.; Krystalvoyager75, 2015), 158.

85. Raymond, "The Caucasian Mind."

fantasy, science fiction, and horror.[86] Only white people are capable of creating science fiction, Raymond asserts, because the white mind alone possesses an imagination that strains to escape "from the only reality that one's eyes saw and one's ears heard."[87] He sets out to prove this through hundreds of pages of praise-singing to whiteness, the sole race that Raymond believes could have created *Frankenstein*, the Harry Potter series, *The Hobbit*, the Earthsea series, *Dune*, "The Sandkings," and "Monster Mash."

Raymond offers several possible explanations for this perceived racial difference. Echoing a long tradition of white nationalist thought, Raymond maintains that the arctic climate of northern Europe selected for the long-term planning associated with food storage and shelter during the winter.[88] However, Raymond argues that inherited prudence does not explain white people's innate love for science fiction.[89] He feels there is something otherworldly about white people, who seem at ease with alternate dimensions, time travel, and universes where time runs at different speeds. Raymond speculates that beings from another planet, habituated to traveling between parallel worlds, passed this yearning to transcend reality down to white humans after mixing with select hominids.[90] He concludes that white people invent science fiction stories because their homeland resides in a different space-time continuum. The idea that white elites are visitors from the future pervades both classic science fiction and far-right speculation.

Genealogies of the Alt-Right

A complete history of the alt-right is beyond the scope of this study, but we can understand the fascist resurgence of the 2010s by placing

86. Raymond, *Sweet Dreams*, 137–38, 159–60, 170–71.
87. Raymond, 159.
88. Raymond, "The Caucasian Mind."
89. Raymond, "The Caucasian Mind."
90. Raymond, *Sweet Dreams*, 347–49.

it in the context of a period characterized by economic stagnation, political paralysis, imperial decline, and cultural exhaustion. This decade produced a recruiting pool of young white men who were internet-obsessed, overeducated, and unhappy with their dwindling prospects in the wake of the financial meltdown.[91] Some of them tried to break this impasse through involvement in Occupy Wall Street, Anonymous, or the Ron Paul Revolution, only to see these movements apparently defeated. They felt trapped in an intolerant present with no future ahead of them.[92]

Under these circumstances they could have just as easily broken for the left, but they were invested with a socially conditioned sense of entitlement that pulled them to the right. Many alt-right partisans began as aspirants for the professional-managerial class but slipped into less prestigious career tracks. Burdened with what I have called the "spoiled cultural capital" of their unrewarded pedigree, training, and credentials, they felt robbed of the chance to exercise their full potential.[93] They were the gifted white boys who, having been promised greatness, came to fetishize this unrealized aptitude as a racial endowment.

Although many alt-right recruits were initially sympathetic to mainstream right-wing ideologies, some felt that the neoconservative-neoliberal project of universalizing liberal capitalist democracy was doomed to failure because it attempted to impose an inherently white system on racial populations unsuited to it.[94] Others simply dropped their professed commitments to economic

---

91. Dale Beran, *It Came from Something Awful: How a Toxic Troll Army Accidentally Memed Donald Trump into Office* (New York: All Points Books, 2019).

92. Beran, *It Came*, 12–16; Mathias Nilges, *Right-Wing Culture in Contemporary Capitalism: Regression and Hope in a Time without Future* (New York: Bloomsbury, 2020), 8–10.

93. Jordan S. Carroll, *Reading the Obscene: Transgressive Editors and the Class Politics of U.S. Literature* (Stanford, Calif.: Stanford University Press, 2021), 188.

94. Main, *Rise of the Alt-Right*, 4, 119–20, 168.

or political liberty to adopt an unapologetic authoritarianism. At the same time, we shouldn't think of the alt-right as a clean break with the mainstream right: there's always been overlap between respectable conservatives, fringe ultraconservatives, and right-wing extremists.[95] Nevertheless, the alt-right still differs from the GOP's reformist line insofar as it calls for a revolutionary program to overthrow existing governments and implement a white ethnostate or imperium that would better protect hierarchies of race, class, religion, and gender.[96]

The alt-right's temporal orientation reflects these revolutionary attitudes. Emma Planinc argues that alt-right hopes to disprove liberal democracy's triumphalist "end of history" narrative by inaugurating a "regenerated future" in which superhuman elites rule unhampered by egalitarianism or liberal humanism.[97] Alexandra Minna Stern describes the alt-right as a project to take white people "back to the future," invoking a paradoxical temporality that rejects linear notions of time as a product of progressive ideology.[98] Because many on the alt-right believe that history moves in cycles and great men can revive ancient archetypes as if no time has passed, they see no contradiction between combining archaic and futuristic elements to make "archeofuturism."[99] Alt-right partisans seek to escape from the current degenerate age and initiate a qualitatively different epoch characterized by both a resurrection of traditional principles *and* a renaissance of technoscientific innovation.

95. John S. Huntington, *Far-Right Vanguard: The Radical Roots of Modern Conservatism* (Philadelphia: University of Pennsylvania Press, 2021), 9–10.

96. Matthew N. Lyons, *Insurgent Supremacists: The U.S. Far Right's Challenge to State and Empire* (Montreal: Kersplebedeb, 2018), ii.

97. Emma Planinc, "Regeneration on the Right: Visions of the Future, Past, and Present," in *Contemporary Far-Right Thinkers and the Future of Liberal Democracy,* ed. A. James McAdams and Alejandro Castrillon (New York: Routledge, 2022), 269–70.

98. Minna Stern, *Proud Boys and the White Ethnostate,* 33.

99. Minna Stern, 35–42.

We might think of the alt-right as regrounding conservative ideas about the future in blood and soil. Melinda Cooper shows that the right turns on a politics of speculative futurity: neoliberals anticipate innovations made possible by speculative finance, neoconservatives forestall emergent threats through preemptive warfare, and evangelicals await the hope embodied in the fetal subject.[100] Each of these future orientations depend on a faith that can risk everything because it believes in pledges made by the free market, the American empire, and God almighty. The alt-right evokes the same anticipatory affects found in GOP politics—techno-optimism, xenophobic paranoia, solicitude for the unborn—but it places its trust instead in the promissory value of the white race.

The alt-right's dreams of unspent potential are clearly framed in generic terms. Spencer speculates that all the "bad-ass men" of the white race who may be imprisoned, opioid-addicted, suicidal, and alcoholic now would've achieved greatness if they'd been given a *Star Trek*–like space program to motivate them.[101] The alt-right converts mediated their grievances through the temporal forms of repetition and variation that have characterized the mass cultural genre system since its inception.[102] Mass cultural media promise familiar novelties: a superhero launches into new adventures even as he remains essentially the same character inhabiting a recognizably similar world.[103] By the same token, fascism portrays the white race as the unchanging protagonist of history even as it ushers in a radically renovated future. The alt-right came to see the world

100. Melinda Cooper, *Life as Surplus: Biotechnology and Capitalism in the Neoliberal Era* (Seattle: University of Washington Press, 2008), 10–14.

101. Free Bird Media Canada, "Richard Spencer—Could Focusing on a Space Program Restore Fire to the Soul of Western Man?" *YouTube*, 4:38, September 20, 2018, https://www.youtube.com/watch?v=w89NOZjBgGQ&ab_channel=FreeBirdMediaCanada.

102. John Rieder, *Science Fiction and the Mass Cultural Genre System* (Middletown, Conn.: Wesleyan University Press, 2017), 57.

103. Umberto Eco, "The Myth of Superman," *Diacritics* 2, no. 1 (Spring 1972): 14–22.

as if governed by a media franchise's canon, possessing a fundamental ethnoracial continuity running underneath every historical difference.

The alt-right therefore has no desire to see a fundamental rupture with present-day identities or hierarchies. They follow the reactionary's motto set forth in Giuseppe di Lampedusa's *The Leopard*: "If we want things to stay as they are, things will have to change."[104] Spencer articulated the metaphysical premises of this historical perspective in his Nietzschean slogan, "become who we are."[105] Unable to countenance real revolution, the alt-right sees tomorrow as the unfolding of possibilities already latent within the white race. For white nationalists, the future is already here.

104. Giuseppe di Lampedusa, *The Leopard,* trans. Archibald Colquhoun (New York: Pantheon, 1960), 40. See also Robin, *Reactionary Mind,* 24.

105. Tamir Bar-On, "Richard B. Spencer and the Alt-Right," in *Key Thinkers of the Radical Right: Behind the New Threat to Liberal Democracy,* ed. Mark Sedgwick (New York: Oxford University Press, 2019), 224.

1. Invaders from the Future

NICK LAND, the intellectual godfather of the Neoreactionary movement, maintains a deep engagement with both science fiction and white supremacist politics. In an infamous post titled "Revenge of the Nerds," Land divides humanity up into two antagonistic groups: "nerds" and "the masses."[1] The "obsolescing" masses resent nerds even as they are forced to depend on their skill in a postindustrial world where "nerd competence is the only economic resource that matters much anymore."[2] Nerds, on the other hand, do not need the masses because they are in the process of automating the kind of drudge work performed by the unintelligent. "Psycho-sadistic girls," "extractive mobs," and "tyrannical politicians" really do not provide much for the nerds "except social torture, parasitism, and bullying."[3] Land's nerds therefore have no interest in dialogue outside of their "productive networks," and increasingly they devote themselves to silent interactions with machines that match or exceed them in rationality.[4] Borrowing terms from Albert O. Hirschman, Land claims that nerds would rather "exit" society than

---

1. Nick Land, "Revenge of the Nerds," *Outside In: Involvements with Reality*, March 21, 2014, https://web.archive.org/web/20140322073447/http://www.xenosystems.net/revenge-of-the-nerds/.
2. Land.
3. Land.
4. Land.

"voice" their objections in democratic debate with people who do not understand them.[5] The nerd imagination is gripped by secessionist utopias such as Galt's Gulch, seasteads, and lunar colonies.[6]

Land claims that nerds are the "final-phase human culture" preparing to break away from earth to become a separate posthuman species.[7] Elsewhere he predicts that space colonization will exert a strong eugenic tendency, selecting only the best and the brightest nerds to produce a superior, space-based race endowed with "the right stuff."[8] Eventually these pressures will evolve Loonies into inhuman creatures ready "to go full Vogon" on their former home planet: *The Moon is a Harsh Mistress* meets *Starship Troopers.*"[9] He thinks this new lifeform will be horrifically alien as well as hostile to *homo sapiens*: "Think face tentacles."[10]

Land refers to Gregory Cochran in his discussions of space eugenics, which is especially apt given Cochran's work with Henry Harpending in *The 10,000 Year Explosion: How Civilization Accelerated Human Evolution* (2009). Borrowing imagery from

5. Albert O. Hirschman, *Exit, Voice, and Loyalty: Responses to Decline in Firms, Organizations, and States* (Cambridge, Mass.: Harvard University Press, 1970), 3–5.

6. Raymond B. Craib, *Adventure Capitalism: A History of Libertarian Exit, from the Era of Decolonization to the Digital Age* (Oakland, Calif.: PM Press, 2022).

7. Land, "Revenge of the Nerds."

8. Gregory Cochran qtd in Nick Land, "Hyper-Racism," *Outside In: Involvements with Reality*, September 29, 2014, https://web.archive.org/web/20211127200915/https://www.xenosystems.net/hyper-racism/.

9. Nick Land, "Lure of the Void, Part 3A," *That's Shanghai*, September 29, 2012, https://web.archive.org/web/20130629145658/http://www.thatsmags.com/shanghai/blog/view/9739. Nick Land, "Lure of the Void, Part 2," *That's Shanghai*, September 6, 2012, https://web.archive.org/web/20121014161640/http://www.thatsmags.com/shanghai/article/2694/lure-of-the-void-part-2.

10. Emphasis deleted. Nick Land, "The Dark Enlightenment (Part 4f(inal))," *That's Shanghai,* July 20, 2012, https://web.archive.org/web/20120726012138/http://www.thatsmags.com/shanghai/article/2497/the-dark-enlightenment-part-4final.

pulp magazines, the coauthors suggest that human evolutionary history "looks more and more like a science fiction novel in which mutants repeatedly arise and displace normal humans—sometimes quietly, simply by surviving, sometimes as a conquering horde."[11] Reiterating this sensational tone throughout their book, Cochran and Harpending recount the colonization of the Americas by disease-resistant Northern Europeans, whom they call "invaders from the future."[12] Cochran and Harpending argue that mutants from populations with a long history of agriculture evolved lower time preferences, i.e., the tendency to value goods expected in the future almost as much as ones available right now.[13] Low time preference allows individuals to postpone gratification and save for tomorrow rather than squandering everything in the present. Cochran and Harpending contrast the "bourgeois virtues" of Eurasian agriculturalists with the "lazy" egalitarianism of people from foraging societies, who they say immediately share or consume everything they produce.[14] Low time preference and other genetic advantages, they argue, contributed to the greater scientific inventiveness of white Europeans compared to people from sub-Saharan Africa or the Islamic world.[15]

Land's work draws upon this same science fictional discourse when he paints geek elites as futuristic mutants. While Land claims that nerds are the next step in evolution, he presents the masses as prehuman throwbacks who have little or nothing "to offer the future."[16] Land repeatedly refers to the masses as monkeys or apes, characterizing them as a brutish species enthralled by instant grat-

11. Gregory Cochran and Henry Harpending, *The 10,000 Year Explosion: How Civilization Accelerated Human Evolution* (New York: Basic Books, 2009), 82.
12. Cochran and Harpending, 164.
13. Cochran and Harpending, 117.
14. Cochran and Harpending, 113–18.
15. Cochran and Harpending, 127.
16. Land, "Revenge of the Nerds."

ification and sublimated sexual status competition.[17] In his "Dark Enlightenment" manifesto, Land argues that democracy makes politicians pander to the masses until there is nothing left of civilization except a "convulsive feeding frenzy."[18] (The cannibalistic zombie horde serves as his favorite image for the demos.) Here Land is clearly influenced by Hans-Hermann Hoppe, a paleolibertarian and Austrian school economist famous for claiming that democracies' tendency toward welfare-statism makes them more primitive, uncivilized, and shortsighted compared to monarchies or anarcho-capitalist societies.[19] Land is equally antidemocratic. He thinks the masses do not possess the low time preference required to build and maintain a technological civilization: they want everything now, making them enemies of both capital accumulation and innovation, which require sacrifice, savings, and patience to achieve.[20]

Land borrows from the most timeworn white supremacist rhetoric to depict the masses in racialized terms. They are hedonistic, hypersexual, unintelligent, and violent, smashing a civilization they do not understand even as they demand more welfare handouts. Land may break with doctrinaire white nationalists insofar as he welcomes high-socioeconomic-status East Asians into his elite, for example, but he converges with them on anti-Blackness. According to Land, his geeks are smart enough to notice Black criminality but

17. Nick Land, "Monkey Business," *Outside In: Involvements with Reality*, November 24, 2013, https://web.archive.org/web/20131127053347/http://www.xenosystems.net/monkey-business/.

18. Nick Land, "The Dark Enlightenment, Part 1," *That's Shanghai*, March 2, 2012, https://web.archive.org/web/20121114085845/http://www.thatsmags.com/shanghai/article/1880/the-dark-enlightenment-part-1.

19. Alexandra Minna Stern, *Proud Boys and the White Ethnostate: How the Alt-Right Is Warping the American Imagination* (Boston: Beacon Press, 2019), 44; Hans-Hermann Hoppe, *Democracy—The God That Failed: The Economics and Politics of Monarchy, Democracy, and Natural Order* (2001; repr. New York: Routledge, 2017), 17–33.

20. Land, "The Dark Enlightenment, Part 1."

lack the empathy and agreeableness to keep quiet about it.[21] Land's nerds turn out to be engaging in white flight when they leave the planet and the human species.

Land typifies a reactionary current that stretches back to science fiction culture's early years. Disaffected science fiction fans have long claimed membership in an advanced race of future-oriented mutants, posthumans, and mad geniuses responsible for the greatest inventions. These nerds believe they inhabit larger timescales and plan farther ahead thanks to their disciplined foresight, but for all their megalomania they feel unappreciated. Science fiction appealed to this sense of geek ressentiment with narratives in which innovators are enslaved by the present-oriented ingrates who need them to run technological society. As in paleolibertarian and white supremacist thought, many popular science fiction narratives suggest that future-orientation is a fixed genetic trait inherited only by a select few. When who counts as a true fan becomes a racial question, the answers often exclude people of color.

Fans are Slans

Geek supremacy dates at least as far back as the heyday of John W. Campbell Jr.'s pulp magazine *Astounding Science Fiction* (later *Analog Science Fiction and Fact*). Science fiction readers during the midcentury period often joked that they were the next stage of evolution. "Fans are slans," they would say, referencing the advanced race of mutants in A. E. van Vogt's *Slan* (1940).[22] What Brian Stableford and David Langford call "mutational romances" allowed

21. Nick Land, "The Dark Enlightenment, Part 4b," *That's Shanghai*, May 3, 2012, https://web.archive.org/web/20120514163626/http://thatsmags.com/shanghai/article/2159/the-dark-enlightenment-part-4b.

22. Andrew Pilsch, "Self-Help Supermen: The Politics of Fan Utopias in World War II–Era Science Fiction," *Science Fiction Studies* 41, no. 3 (November 2014): 526.

science fiction fans to reimagine themselves as members of a superior species that would someday rule the world.[23]

Some science fiction fans adopted these attitudes with enthusiasm. Van Vogt's *Slan* encouraged readers to identify with its protagonist, and soon fans gathered in communal houses or "Slan Shacks" where they enjoyed the company of like-minded individuals who half-jokingly claimed to possess superior intelligence.[24] Other fans called for a self-contained intentional community they called the "Slan Center."[25] Claude Degler went even further to develop an ideology he termed "fanationalism."[26] He spent much of the 1940s calling on fans to retreat to a rural compound in the Ozarks where they'd initiate a eugenics program, breeding science fiction enthusiasts together to produce a race of supermen or "Homo Cosmens" who'd rise up to build a new civilization.[27] The Cosmen's defining feature was the unlimited scope of their interests, including an appreciation for boundless reaches of space and time.[28] Although Degler claimed that fans aren't limited by race, he suggested they're born as a result of genetic mutations.[29] They are what H. G. Wells called the "Star-Begotten," the vanguard of a new species that will supersede *homo sapiens*.[30]

Backlash against Degler came swiftly. Mutational romances had long taken pains to distance themselves from the master-race con-

23. Brian M Stableford and David Langford, "Mutants," *The Encyclopedia of Science Fiction,* September 13, 2021, https://sf-encyclopedia .com/entry/mutants. See also Colin Milburn, "Posthumanism," *The Oxford Handbook of Science Fiction,* ed. Rob Latham, 524–36 (New York: Oxford University Press, 2014).

24. Brian Attebery, "Super Men," *Science Fiction Studies* 25, no. 1 (March 1998): 64. Pilsch, "Self Help Superman," 529.

25. Pilsch, "Self Help Superman," 530.

26. Pilsch, 536.

27. Pilsch, 538.

28. Claude Degler, "Announcement of Cosmic Fandom and the Cosmic Circle," *Cosmic Circle Monthly* 1, no. 1 (June 1944): 5, https://fanac .org/fanzines/Cosmic_Circle_Pubs/Cosmic_Circle29.pdf.

29. Degler, 6.

30. Degler, 3.

cept promoted by fascism, and many fans were revolted by selective breeding's affinity with Nazism.[31] (Degler's public profile was also hurt by rumors of statutory rape and institutionalization.) Despite this widespread ridicule, Degler's ideas clearly appealed to some fans: James H. Madole, whom we encountered in the Introduction, shared the same dream.

Fannish elitism was common in the science fiction community. While science fiction fans and their mutant analogues often claimed superiority based on intelligence, many prided themselves in inhabiting larger temporal horizons than regular human beings.[32] During his guest of honor speech at the third World Science Fiction Convention in 1941, Robert A. Heinlein argued that "science fiction fans differ from most of the rest of the race by thinking in terms of racial magnitudes—not even centuries, but thousands of years."[33]

Mutational romances reflected these ideas by presenting posthuman protagonists who think and act on a grand scale. *Slan* especially emphasizes this trait, depicting mutants capable of executing plans that take a hundred years to fulfill.[34] Slans aren't alone in possessing the gift of foresight: mutants in other novels cast their minds forward through time or use their supernormal longevities to carry out longer-term projects than any baseline human could achieve.[35] Most of van Vogt's novel is devoted to a series of plots and counterplots orchestrated by slans over many years, all of which

31. Pilsch, "Supermen," 539. H. G. Wells, *Star-Begotten* (1937; repr. New York: Manor Books, 1975), 132, 138–39; Olaf Stapledon, *Odd John* (1936; repr. New York: Garland Publishing, 1975), 76–78; Robert A. Heinlein, *Beyond This Horizon* (1942; repr. New York: Baen, 2002), 87–88, 157–58; James Blish, *Jack of Eagles* (1952; repr. New York: Avon, 1982), 113–15; Robert A. Heinlein, *Methuselah's Children* (New York: Signet, 1958), 42–43.

32. Milburn, "Posthumanism," 525.

33. Robert A. Heinlein, "Guest of Honor Speech at the Third World Science Fiction Convention—Denver, 1941," *Requiem: New Collected Works by Robert A. Heinlein and Tributes to the Grand Master*, ed. Yoji Kondo (New York: Tor, 1992), 155.

34. A. E. Van Vogt, *Slan* (1940; repr. New York: Tor, 2007), 159.

35. Stapledon, *Odd John*, 130–32. Heinlein, *Methuselah's Children*, 50.

are ultimately subsumed into a vast conspiracy to save the slan race that unfolds over centuries. The slan protagonists exemplify what Ursula K. Le Guin would later call the "the linear, progressive, Time's-(killing)-arrow mode of the Techno-Heroic," pursuing distant narrative goals with the efficient path of a ranged weapon.[36]

If mutants are the future in these narratives, baseline humans represent the past. *Slan* likens them to "the Java ape man, the Neanderthal beast man, and the Cro-Magnon primitive."[37] As John Rieder has shown, early science fiction such as alien invasion and lost world narratives figured colonial relations as anachronistic encounters between societies or species inhabiting vastly different stages of technological development.[38] Mutational romances transpose the temporal logic of these subgenres onto differences within American or European populations, positing a futuristic elect who no longer shares a common history with the living fossils that make up the popular majority.[39] Because normies dwell in the past, they find it difficult to participate in a mutual dialogue with mutants, let alone work together with them in a shared political project.[40]

Mutants in these narratives therefore tend to choose exit over voice, forming separatist enclaves or secret societies to pursue their interests without having to explain themselves to people who do not understand them.[41] Wells's Star-Begotten avoid politics and choose instead to deal with problems in "material science and mechanical invention," where mutants can achieve success through practical results not easily discounted by inferior intellects.[42] His characters

36. Ursula K. Le Guin, "The Carrier Bag Theory of Fiction," in *Dancing at the Edge of the World* (1986; repr New York: Grove, 1989), 170.

37. Van Vogt, *Slan.* 251–52.

38. John Rieder, *Colonialism and the Emergence of Science Fiction* (Middletown, Conn.: Wesleyan University Press, 2008), 5–6.

39. See Rieder, 78–80.

40. See Johannes Fabian, *Time and the Other: How Anthropology Makes Its Object* (New York: Columbia University Press, 1983), 31.

41. See, for example, Stapledon, *Odd John*, 150–57.

42. H. G. Wells, *Star-Begotten* (1937; repr. New York: Manor Books, 1975), 124–25.

predict that someday the Star-Begotten may need to assert themselves by withdrawing their technical abilities from baseline tyrants,
allowing society to crumble.[43]

Ever changeable, the figure of the mutant has been utilized for
left-wing causes as well as for right.[44] Mutants frequently appear
as marginalized misfits rather than masterminds, and overconfi-
dently masculine superhuman narratives later found a feminist
rejoinder in superwoman stories.[45] However, for all the mutational
romance's political complexities, reactionaries such as Madole and
Land are drawn to the simplified image of the forward-looking few
who triumph over the backwards many. Although the authors of
many mutational romances undercut fascist readings of their texts—
Stapledon describes Odd John and his posthuman companions as
nonwhite, for example—the far right relies on creative misreadings
when it suits their purposes.[46]

Nevertheless, mutants and other "pariah elites" possess an
ideological flexibility that makes them useful for the far right.[47]
Mutational romances often characterize democracy as a tyranny of
the majority that oppresses the exceptional individuals who are im-

43. Wells, *Star-Begotten,* 143–45.

44. Sean Cashbaugh, "A Paradoxical, Discrepant, Mutant Marxism:
Imagining a Radical Science Fiction in the American Popular Front,"
Journal for the Study of Radicalism 10, no. 1 (Spring 2016): 63–10; Ramzi
Fawaz, *The New Mutants: Superheroes and the Radical Imagination of
American Comics* (New York: New York University Press, 2016); Andrew
Pilsch, *Transhumanism: Evolutionary Futurism and the Human Technologies
of Utopia* (Minneapolis: University of Minnesota Press, 2017); Colin
Milburn, "Mutate or Die: Neo-Lamarckian Ecogames and Responsible
Evolution," *Ecogames,* eds. Laura op de Beke, Gerald Farca, Joost Raessens,
and Stefan Werning (Amsterdam: Amsterdam University Press, 2022).

45. Brian Attebery, *Decoding Gender in Science Fiction* (New York:
Routledge, 2002), 82–105.

46. Stapledon, *Odd John,* 9, 159.

47. David Langford, "Pariah Elite," *The Encyclopedia of Science Fiction,*
eds. John Clute and David Langford (London: SFE/Ansible Editions, 2015),
https://sf-encyclopedia.com/entry/pariah_elite.

mune to "mass emotions," "crowd loyalties," and "herd influences."[48] Paradoxically they hint that mutants are most fit to rule the masses precisely because they are anti-totalitarian. This move gives reactionaries a pretext to claim liberty, toleration, and progress in the name of an authoritarian political program. When mutants embark on a quest for world domination as in *Slan*, it is to save themselves from the normal humans who want to restrict them from realizing their true potentials. Mutant freedom proves incompatible with baseline democracy.

Perhaps for these reasons *Star Trek* would later reject the mutant figure as antithetical to Starfleet's political principles in the 1967 episode "Space Seed." In it, the crew of the starship Enterprise clashes with the cryogenically revived superhuman dictator Khan Noonien Singh, played by Ricardo Montalbán, who along with his master race ruled over much of Earth during the Eugenics Wars that took place centuries earlier. Khan—who is sexy and aristocratic, styling himself as Milton's Satan—represents an enticing but ultimately rejected alternative to the crew's socialist values. Unsurprisingly, then, Khan is the only *Star Trek* character beloved by Richard Spencer. He glosses over the villain's mixed racial heritage, presenting him as a Nietzschean superman whose Aryan spirit allows him to stand against the Jewish and Marxist egalitarianism embodied in Mr. Spock.[49]

Superhumans are a longstanding obsession for Spencer, who often reads science fiction against the grain to find superior beings to admire. He is thrilled by Bond villain Hugo Drax in *Moonraker* (1979), who plots to release poison gases into Earth's atmosphere and repopulate the planet with "new god men" hidden on his space

---

48. Wells, *Star-Begotten*, 94, 143, 151. See also David M. Higgins, *Reverse Colonization: Science Fiction, Imperial Fantasy, and Alt-Victimhood* (Iowa City: University of Iowa Press, 2021), 37.

49. Richard Spencer, Colin Lidell, and Andy Nowicki, "Nerd Socialism," *Vanguard Radio*, Podcast Audio, May 20, 2013, https://archive .org/details/NerdSocialism.

station, and he hails the posthuman replicants of *Blade Runner* (1982) as awesome "Aryan-like figures" in an "Asiatic, decrepit world of ant people."[50] Spencer even imagines that Arnold Schwarzenegger's Terminator is "an Austrian Nazi coming to us from the future," representing a "superman" produced by eugenics who is "as far away from us as we are from the great apes."[51] In this bizarre reading, the Terminator traveled to the past to revise history by killing Jews, but he is ultimately reprogrammed by "white guilt" to commit (racial) suicide.[52] Spencer's antisemitism leads him to worry over what he sees as the cooptation of the Übermensch figure by the Jewish creators of *Superman* comics, Jerry Siegel and Joe Schuster, and he wonders if it's possible to recuperate the Man of Steel for white gentiles.[53] All the ambivalences of the mutational romance seem to disappear in Spencer's superhuman power fantasies.

"A Cannibal of the Moment"

Mutational romances explore how the self-appointed geek elite feels exploited by people who do not match them in intelligence or foresight. For example, Jommy Cross, the mutant protagonist of *Slan,* is enslaved by an unevolved human named Granny. While Jommy works to further his dead father's long-range plan to save

50. Many alt-right podcasts have been removed from mainstream platforms. Whenever I could not locate a version of the podcast audio referenced in this book on a stable, reputable, and freely accessible website, I have cited the version kept in my personal archive. Richard Spencer and Mark Brahmin, "Unconscious Cinema—Goldeneye," *Radix*, podcast audio, December 30, 2020, author's archive; Richard Spencer and Mark Brahmin, "Unconscious Cinema—Less Human Than Human," *Radix*, podcast audio, October 29, 2017, author's archive.

51. Richard Spencer and Mark Brahmin, "Unconscious Cinema—The Terminator," *Radix*, podcast audio, August 9, 2017, author's archive.

52. Spencer and Brahmin, "Unconscious Cinema—The Terminator."

53. Richard Spencer and Mark Brahmin, "Superchrist—Unconscious Cinema: Man of Steel (2013)," *Radix*, podcast audio, March 30, 2021, author's archive.

the slans, his captor pursues more immediate goals. The childishly impulsive Granny profits from Jommy's psychic powers by forcing him to steal things to fund her lavish consumption. When Granny's chaotic actions threaten his utopian project, leaving "his future abruptly blank, unplanned, homeless," Jommy must save them both from the consequences of her ill-considered decisions.[54] Unable to take care of herself, she ends the novel as Jommy's happy, hypnotized slave. Order is restored once she submits to the mutant's grand designs.

We can understand these stories as akin to what David M. Higgins calls "alt-victimhood," political fantasies and science fiction plots wherein the dominant group of white men find themselves victimized by people who are oppressed in the real world.[55] These include "reverse colonization" narratives in which white colonizers somehow become colonized subordinates.[56] Although reverse colonization has sometimes served as a call for solidarity with the oppressed, more often this trope merely enables reactionaries including members of the alt-right to pose as victims, an "imperial masochism" that affords them both self-pitying pleasure and moral righteousness.[57]

Higgins finds this in more mainstream science fiction ranging from *Star Wars* to Philip K. Dick, but we can also see reverse colonization at work in nativist and white nationalist narratives. Jean Raspail's *The Camp of the Saints* (1973)—a favorite of Steve Bannon—describes the destruction of Europe by a monstrous flotilla of Indian refugees. Raspail figures the migrants as a "mob of Martians" and "an army of little green men from some remote planet"—alien invaders who have nothing in common with the Europeans they despoil.[58] His novel served as a key influence for Renaud Camus, whose con-

---

54. Van Vogt, *Slan*, 117.
55. Higgins, *Reverse Colonization*, 23.
56. Higgins, 1–3.
57. Higgins, 2.
58. Jean Raspail, *The Camp of the Saints*, trans. Norman Shapiro (1973, repr. Petoskey, Mich.: Social Contract Press, 1987), 50, 260.

spiracy theory that white people are being "replaced" by nonwhite Muslim immigrants inspired the 2019 Christchurch mosque shootings.[59] These ideas have also fed into the white-genocide narratives including race war novels such as Kyle Bristow's *White Apocalypse* (2010). Reverse colonization has become a powerful propaganda tool for the white power movement.

Mainstream science fiction tends to approach white supremacy from a somewhat more oblique angle. As I shall show in the following section, science fiction authors including C. M. Kornbluth, Ayn Rand, Robert A. Heinlein, Larry Niven, and Jerry Pournelle have staged alt-victimhood narratives in which future-oriented workers and entrepreneurs are threatened with bondage and cannibalism by a racialized class of present-oriented parasites. These narratives maintain deep roots in a right-wing ideology that Chip Berlet and Matthew N. Lyons term producerism, "a doctrine that champions the so-called producers in society against both 'unproductive' elites and subordinate groups defined as lazy and immoral."[60] Unlike the populist forms of producerism prevalent during the Trump era, the narratives examined here argue that the real producers aren't manual workers but instead the gifted minds who originate new products and methods of production.[61] Without this small minority of geniuses, they suggest, society would collapse.

C. M. Kornbluth's "The Marching Morons" is an early instance of this tendency in science fiction. A normal man finds himself in a

59. Sasha Polakow-Suransky, "The Inspiration for Terrorism in New Zealand Came From France," *Foreign Policy,* March 16, 2019, https://foreignpolicy.com/2019/03/16/the-inspiration-for-terrorism-in-new-zealand-came-from-france-christchurch-brenton-tarrant-renaud-camus-jean-raspail-identitarians-white-nationalism/.

60. Chip Berlet and Matthew N. Lyons, *Right-Wing Populism in America: Too Close for Comfort* (New York: Guilford, 2018), 6.

61. See Richard J. Herrnstein and Charles Murray, *The Bell Curve: Intelligence and Class Structure in American Life* (New York: Free Press, 1991), 54–61; David Duke, *My Awakening* (Covington, LA: Free Speech Press, 1999), 651.

distant future where he is more intelligent than most citizens. We're informed that the average IQ dropped to 45 thanks to a dysgenic trend that started because "economic and social conditions . . . penalized child-bearing by the prudent and foresighted."[62] Sensible people who practiced family planning produced relatively few offspring, while "the migrant workers, slum dwellers, and tenant farmers were shiftlessly and short-sightedly having children—breeding, breeding. My God, how they bred!"[63] The remaining cognitive elite keeps society going for the so-called morons, who effectively treat them like "slaves."[64] As one smarty puts it, "millions of workers live in luxury on the sweat of the handful of aristocrats."[65]

The narrative makes clear that racial degeneration has degraded executive function more than abstract reasoning. In the first scene we meet a potter who serves as a prime example of the dwindling intelligentsia. What marks him as such is not his mathematical or verbal aptitude but, rather, his ability to wait for his pottery to fire.[66] He successfully overcomes the desire to open his kiln to check on the progress of his pottery, a move that would risk shattering his creation. Delaying gratification, he further demonstrates his providence by prospecting for copper to use in later ceramics projects. By contrast, his buyer nearly spends his entire budget all at once before his gifted secretary talks him out of it. This suggests that the ability to save and prepare for the future has been bred out of all but the eugenically selected.

Heedless of consequences, the shortsighted masses overpopulate the planet and begin consuming all its resources. At first the cognitive elite attempts to eliminate the impulsivists by withdrawing to the South Pole, allowing civilization to collapse into famine and

62. C. M. Kornbluth, "The Marching Morons" (1951), reprinted in *The Best of C. M. Kornbluth*, ed. Frederik Pohl (New York: Taplinger Publishing, 1976), 149.

63. Kornbluth, 149.

64. Kornbluth, 150.

65. Kornbluth, 148.

66. Kornbluth, 133–35.

war, but after a few disastrous weeks they realize that letting their inferiors die would leave them with five billion bodies to clean up.[67] They eventually solve this problem by shooting all intellectually disabled people into space in rockets designed as death traps, a program suggested by the visitor from the past's recollections of Hitler.[68] The cognitive elite feel regret afterward and execute him for proposing it.

The story's politics are complicated, especially given the author's membership in the left-leaning Futurians. It operates through irony and paradox, satirizing both ruthless intellectuals and the unintelligent citizens they murder in a program of mass killing that appears as simultaneously monstrous and necessary to preserve civilization.[69] Nevertheless, in subsequent decades Kornbluth's short story became a touchstone for scientific racists who failed to acknowledge its ambiguities.[70] Unsurprisingly, they prefer the one-dimensional version of the narrative found in *Idiocracy* (2006), one of the alt-right's favorite films.[71]

Understood in this light, Kornbluth's title is as precise as it is odious. Henry H. Goddard, a central figure in the history of eugenics, coined the term "moron" to describe an adult with a mental age of between eight and twelve years who, possessed with a "defective mentality" since birth or childhood, proves to be "in-

67. Kornbluth, 150.

68. Kornbluth, 153.

69. John Huntington, *Rationalizing Genius: Ideological Strategies in the Classic American Science Fiction Story* (New Brunswick, N.J.: Rutgers University Press, 1989), 64.

70. Steve Sailer, "Idiocracy: The Morons Shall Inherit the Earth," *The Unz Review*, October 6, 2006, https://web.archive.org/web/20221111092128/https://www.unz.com/isteve/idiocracy/; Gregory Cochran, "Live Not by Lies," *West Hunter*, April 8, 2018, https://web.archive.org/web/20240328101152/https://westhunt.wordpress.com/2018/04/08/live-not-by-lies/.

71. Howe Abbott-Hiss, "Why We're Getting Dumber," *Counter-Currents*, February 14, 2019, https://web.archive.org/web/20240301041847/https://counter-currents.com/2019/02/why-were-getting-dumber/.

capable of competing in the struggle for existence or of managing his own affairs with ordinary prudence."[72] According to Goddard, a "high-grade moron" can perform many of the tasks within the grasp of a normal individual, but they are "unable to plan."[73] Stanley Porteus, Goddard's successor at the Vineland Training School for Feebleminded Children, drew upon these ideas when he developed a test to measure "prudence, forethought, planning capacity, ability to improve with practice, and adaptability to a new situation."[74] He used this diagnostic instrument to rank nonwhite races as inferior and reaffirm settler-colonial control by supposedly demonstrating that many nonwhite populations including Filipinos and Native Hawaiians were incapable of governing themselves.[75] By invoking Goddard's terminology, Kornbluth implicates the narrative's elite in a long history of racist and eugenicist thinking about hereditary differences in foresight.

Rand's *Atlas Shrugged* (1957) pursues the same theme of a genius minority swamped by imbeciles, but it does so with a much more earnest and didactic tone. Rand's dystopian novel is best known for sending many young people down the path of free market capitalism. It features a small elite of capitalist entrepreneurs who resist the redistributive state's parasitism by withdrawing to a secret enclave called Atlantis or Galt's Gulch, where they watch as civilization folds without their help. This libertarian utopia's residents are bound together by a strong work ethic, individu-

72. Henry H. Goddard, "Who Is a Moron?" *The Scientific Monthly* 21, no. 1 (January 1927), 42–43.

73. Henry H. Goddard qtd in Richard A. Berry and Stanley Porteus, *Intelligence and Social Valuation: A Practical Method for Diagnosis of Mental Deficiency and Other Forms of Social Inefficiency* (Vineland, N.J.: The Training School at Vineland Jersey, 1920), 67.

74. Goddard, 91.

75. David E. Stannard, "Honoring Racism: The Professional Life and Reputation of Stanley D. Porteus," in *The Ethnic Studies Story: Politics and Social Movements in Hawai'i: Essays in Honor of Marion Kelly,* ed. Ibrahim G. Aoudé. 95–100 (Honolulu: University of Hawai'i at Mānoa).

alistic principles, and, above all, a shared politics of time. Rand admires entrepreneurs who set a distant goal in the future and strike out for it with a monomaniacal focus.[76] Because these heroic innovators seem to dwell in futurity, a trip to Galt's Gulch seems like a voyage to another world filled with pioneering technology unfathomable to the citizens of the outside world.[77] Despite the antagonism between the two thinkers, Friedrich Hayek imagines something similar when he compares elites to "men on a previously unknown continent or on another planet" who possess an "advanced knowledge" that they may graciously bring to Earth's more backward inhabitants.[78]

Not everyone is fit for Rand's future. Rand labels Indigenous peoples, collectivists, and welfare recipients as "savages" who can never accomplish their goals because they do not understand the laws of causality.[79] Instead of planning for the future, they follow the "expediency of the moment."[80] When they do follow the steps laid out by Promethean inventors, they enact them with "the jerky motions of an ape performing a routine it [has] learned to copy by muscular habit."[81] Because these so-called savages cannot innovate for themselves, they must enslave their future-oriented superiors to invent for them, but once they have achieved this goal technology quickly reverts to prior developmental stages as regulation and taxation stifle entrepreneurial initiative.[82] The savage society can do little more than devour reserves built up by heroic individuals during freer times, consuming capital at the expense of future

76. Ayn Rand, *Atlas Shrugged* (1957; repr. New York: Penguin, 1996), 30, 158.

77. Rand, 1136.

78. Friedrich Hayek, *The Constitution of Liberty: The Definitive Edition* (Chicago: University of Chicago Press, 2011), 100.

79. Rand, *Atlas Shrugged,* 917.

80. Rand, 363, 912, 933.

81. Rand, 560.

82. Rand, 632, 917, 1039.

prosperity. The collectivist becomes "a cannibal of the moment, devouring the unborn children of greatness."[83]

Rand's temporal politics rest on deeply racist assumptions. She patterns her heroes on pulp serials from her childhood reading that feature hypermasculine British explorers with stereotypically Aryan features who dominated and exterminated the natives standing in their way.[84] Throughout *Atlas Shrugged*, Rand racializes the collectivist moochers by calling them "primitive," "tribal," and "Asiatic."[85] As Jessica Hurley demonstrates, the novel presents a paranoid racial fantasy in which "whiteness is a worldly orientation that has sole access to both rationality and futurity," consigning the nonwhite world to "apocalyptic futurelessness."[86]

Rand's racial ideology finds its reflection in the neoliberal economics of the Austrian school. Many neoliberal thinkers insisted that socialism is merely a regression to irrational savagery.[87] Lars Cornelissen shows that early Austrian theorists contrasted the economizing civilized subject favorably against the "futureless savage" who does not bother to construct a shelter before winter, store food in advance, or otherwise anticipate future needs.[88] In this view, capitalist accumulation becomes an expression of racially determined providence.

83. Rand, 335.

84. Lisa Duggan, *Mean Girl: Ayn Rand and the Culture of Greed* (Oakland, Calif.: University of California Press, 2019), 14–15, 43.

85. Rand qtd in Duggan, *Mean Girl,* 60.

86. Jessica Hurley, *Infrastructures of Apocalypse: American Literature and the Nuclear Complex* (Minneapolis: University of Minnesota Press, 2020), 54–55, 32.

87. Jessica Whyte, *The Morals of the Market: Human Rights and the Rise of Neoliberalism* (New York: Verso, 2019), 14, 35–74; Julia Elyachar, "Neoliberalism, Rationality, and the Savage Slot," in *Mutant Neoliberalism: Market Rule and Political Rupture,* eds. William Callison and Zachary Manfredi (New York: Fordham University Press, 2020), 186.

88. Lars Cornelissen, "Savage Economics: Race, Futurity, and Civilizational Hierarchy in Early Austrian Neoliberalism," *Global Perspectives* 2, no. 1 (2021): 4–6.

Atlas Shrugged inspired Ward Kendall's white nationalist science fiction novel *Hold Back This Day* (1999). The novel is set in a future in which a multicultural world government has almost eliminated the white race through clandestine ethnic cleansing operations and near-compulsory miscegenation. State propaganda attributes all technoscientific achievements to Africans, and children are taught that the first astronaut on the moon was a Black woman. But, according to the narrative, innovation has stalled and spaceflight is all but lost because there are so few white technicians and scientists. White people are the "progenitor of human progress," we are told.[89] To underscore this point, the protagonist comes upon a ruined industrial park with a sign that reads, "Reardon Steel: South Africa Division," an allusion to the business destroyed by collectivists in *Atlas Shrugged*.[90] Following John Galt's example, white nationalists secede to a Martian colony before leaving for Alpha Centauri. Driving home the message, one white man says, "we have no possible future left on this world . . . [b]ut there may be a future for our Race *elsewhere*."[91] Once white people are gone, an overpopulated Earth falls into mass starvation and a new Dark Ages begins. Although this novel is relatively recent, the idea that white people possess a technoscientific aptitude absent in people of color can be traced as far back the eighteenth century.[92]

Mainstream science fiction joins Rand in presenting collectivism as racialized. Robert A. Heinlein's *Farnham's Freehold* (1964) depicts a distant future in which a Black ruling class called the Chosen runs a welfare state dependent upon white slaves. Heinlein describes this Black-dominated society as "stable, even static" with

89. Ward Kendall, *Hold Back This Day* (1999; repr. United States: Alternative Future, 2020), 239.

90. Kendall, 89.

91. Kendall, 146.

92. Robert Wald Sussman, *The Myth of Race: The Troubling Persistence of an Unscientific Idea* (Cambridge, Mass.: Harvard University Press, 2014), 26–27.

"few innovations" to its credit.[93] The Chosen culture carries out little scientific research, and most of the breakthroughs it does achieve are discovered by white, castrated slaves, who have little motive to innovate because their ideas are always stolen by Black masters who take all the glory.[94] Even this ingenuity is in short supply because the Chosen breed drive and intelligence out of white slaves in captivity, forcing the Chosen to maintain free populations of rebel whites whose members can be captured to replenish the bloodlines of expert slaves.[95] When a freeborn white man with extraordinary entrepreneurial abilities is teleported from the distant past, he appears as a mutant or a "freak" in this world.[96]

For their part, the Chosen seem incapable of speculation. They see their present order as eternal, their prejudices as natural law, and major changes as impossible.[97] We never meet a Black character in the novel who is as dynamic and imaginative as the white protagonist. As if to literalize Rand's racist metaphor for the redistributive state, Heinlein reveals at the end of the novel that the Chosen are cannibals, devouring the white people they exploit.[98] This theme reappears in Jerry Pournelle and Larry Niven's *Lucifer's Hammer* (1977), in which an army of cannibalistic criminals and hippies led by an impulsive Black race hustler threatens civilizational progress by attacking the survivalists working to rebuild technological society after a comet strikes Earth.[99] Once more, futurity is equated with whiteness while Blackness is relegated to the savage state of the futureless present. This novel was

93. Robert A. Heinlein, *Farnham's Freehold* (New York: G. P. Putnam's Sons, 1964), 177, 205.

94. Heinlein, 225.

95. Heinlein, 285–86.

96. Heinlein, 183.

97. Heinlein, 211.

98. Heinlein, 262.

99. Larry Niven and Jerry Pournelle, *Lucifer's Hammer* (New York: Ballantine, 1977), 73, 528.

nominated for the Hugo Award in 1978. Although it did not win, the tradition it represents would resurface in the 2010s.

Sad Puppies, Rabid Puppies

The Hugo Awards at the World Science Fiction Convention have been one of the signature events of fandom since 1953. Every year fans select the best science fiction and fantasy in categories ranging from best novel to best fanzine. Despite their reputation for populism, the Hugos have often rewarded formally experimental social science fiction with left-leaning politics and countercultural themes: past winners include Alfred Bester, Philip K. Dick, Ursula K. Le Guin, William Gibson, and Octavia Butler. However, in the 2010s the Hugo Awards experienced a right-wing backlash that came to be known as science fiction's GamerGate. A group of conservative fans calling themselves the Sad Puppies ran slates designed to block what they saw as literary fiction penned by "social justice agitators."[100] Promoting a revisionist history of the genre, the Sad Puppies claimed that they were saving science fiction and fantasy from the "literati."[101]

The Sad Puppies were unsuccessful when they were mobilized in 2013 and 2014 by Larry Correia, but after Brad R. Torgersen took over in 2015 they swept the nominations thanks to a coordinated campaign. Although most Worldcon members did not support the Sad Puppies, these opposition votes were divided among too many choices to prevent a small troll army working in lockstep from dictating the Hugo Award nominees. After many weeks of flamewars and some tense moments at Worldcon, protest votes for

100. Brad R. Torgersen qtd in Emily St. James, "How Conservatives Took Over Sci-Fi's Most Prestigious Award," *Vox*, August 22, 2015, https://www.vox.com/2015/4/26/8495415/hugos-sad-puppies-controversy.

101. Larry Correia, "How to Get Correia Nominated for a Hugo. 😊," *Monster Hunter Nation*, January 8, 2013, https://monsterhunternation.com/2013/01/08/how-to-get-correia-nominated-for-a-hugo/.

"No Award" won out over the Sad Puppy picks in most categories. Fandom soundly rejected reaction.

The Sad Puppies presented themselves as sensible and nondoctrinaire. They claimed to oppose political correctness and foster cultural diversity by promoting "unabashed pulp action that isn't heavy-handed message fic."[102] In actuality, the Sad Puppies in 2015 turned out to be little more than a stalking horse for an extreme right-wing faction known as the Rabid Puppies, who were led by alt-right blogger, author, and publisher Theodore Beale (also known as "Vox Day"). Although the Sad Puppy leaders sometimes distanced themselves from Beale, most of the successful Sad Puppy nominations also appeared on the Rabid Puppy slate, suggesting that their campaign may have been another nonstarter without Beale's followers.[103] The Sad Puppies complained they merely wanted to bust up the social justice cliques at Worldcon to make way for more classic genre fiction—the Rabid Puppies hoped to burn the Hugo Awards to the ground.

Beale's journey toward the alt-right began with a regular column for the paleoconservative site WorldNetDaily, where his father served as an investor and board member.[104] Beale's columns regularly espoused Islamophobic and misogynistic opinions, and his antifeminist bona fides allowed him to reinvent himself as a master of pickup artistry, offering sexist dating advice to "involuntary celibate" or "incel" readers.[105] Always a contentious figure, Beale's vendetta against the rest of fan culture can be dated to his failed presidential bid for the Science Fiction and Fantasy Writers

102. Correia, "Nominated," n.p.

103. Elizabeth Sandifer, "Guided by the Beauty of Their Weapons: An Analysis of Theodore Beale and His Supporters," in *Neoreaction a Basilisk: Essays on and around the Alt Right* (Monee, Ill.: Eruditorium Press, 2017), 353.

104. Camestros Felapton, *The Complete Debarkle: 1880–2020* (Sydney, Australia: Cattimothy House, 2021), 28.

105. Felapton, 76.

of America (SFWA) in 2013.[106] Following the election, N. K. Jemisin spoke out against Beale, publicly expressing her dismay that "a self-described misogynist, racist, anti-Semite, and a few other flavors of asshole" could win a tenth of the vote.[107] Beale confirmed her accusation by releasing a volley of racist and sexist tirades on his blog. Beale shared these remarks using the SFWA Twitter account, an action that resulted in his expulsion from the organization.

Beale's comments must be understood within the context of Jemisin's career. Early on Jemisin criticized science fiction "as one of the most racist genres in American literature."[108] Many science fiction novels featured all-white casts of characters, erasing people of color in what amounted to "literary genocide."[109] When she told people that she wrote science fiction, many seemed incredulous that a Black woman would write in the genre. One of her cousins even suggested that science fiction was "white people's stuff."[110] Jemisin devoted herself to proving that science fiction was not inherently white: "I'm always surprised that there aren't more people of color writing in this genre, because the future is *ours*."[111]

Beale's rejoinder to Jemisin's speech proves her critique of the field, othering the author while reaffirming the genre's whiteness:

[u]nlike the white males she excoriates, there is no evidence to be found anywhere on the planet that a society of NK Jemisins is capable of building an advanced civilization, or even successfully maintaining one without significant external support from those white

106. David Forbes, *The Old Iron Dream* (Oakland, Calif.: Inkshares, 2014).

107. N. K. Jemisin, "Continuum GoH Speech," *N. K. Jemisin*, June 8, 2013, https://nkjemisin.com/2013/06/continuum-goh-speech/.

108. N. K. Jemisin, "No More Lily-White Futures and Monochrome Myths," *The Angry Black Woman*, April 21, 2007, http://theangryblackwoman.com/2007/04/21/no-more-lily-white-futures-and-monochrome-myths/.

109. Jemisin, "No More Lily-White Futures."

110. N. K. Jemisin, "Author Statement," *Transcriptase*, accessed October 6, 2022, http://transcriptase.org/statements/nkjemisin/#more-324.

111. Jemisin, "No More Lily-White Futures."

males. If one considers that it took my English and German ancestors more than one thousand years to become fully civilized after their first contact with advanced Greco-Roman civilization, it should be patently obvious that it is illogical to imagine, let alone insist, that Africans have somehow managed to do the same in less than half the time at a greater geographic distance. These things take time.[112]

Beale positions himself here as an emissary of the future, looking backward on Jemisin. He tries to write Jemisin out of the science fiction community by asserting that a Black woman could never build a future world because she is a thousand years behind the white civilizational present. It's clear who won fandom's hearts and minds: Jemisin later earned Hugo Awards three in a row, but Beale's entries repeatedly placed behind "No Award." A stinging rebuke.

Beale's peevish castigation that "these things take time" reflects a dominant racist discourse on temporality that, as Michael Hanchard points out, positions Black populations as lagging or delayed.[113] Because white supremacists demote Black people to a prior stage of development, dooming them to repeat past European accomplishments, they have often been made to wait for the rights and goods white people have long enjoyed. Jemisin's *The Broken Earth* trilogy can be read as the most eloquent response to Beale's white supremacist stalling tactics. The novels' vision of social change defies gradualism, choosing instead to end racialized slavery through an apocalyptic rupture that immediately abolishes the world's predictable rhythms.[114]

112. Theodore Beale [Vox Day], "A Black Female Fantasist Calls for Reconciliation," *Vox Popoli,* June 13, 2013, https://web.archive.org/web/20240419101925/https://voxday.net/2013/06/13/a-black-female-fantasis/.

113. Beale, "A Black Female Fantasist"; Michael Hanchard, "Afro-Modernity: Temporality, Politics, and the African Diaspora," *Public Culture* 11, no. 1 (1999): 251–52.

114. Jesse A. Goldberg, "Demanding the Impossible: Scales of Apocalypse and Abolition Time in N. K. Jemisin's Broken Earth," *ASAP/Journal* 7, no. 3 (September 2022): 640.

Beale's anti-Black racism runs deeper than procrastination in the face of racial inequality. In another post, Beale explains that when he suggested that native-born English and Germans are more civilized than Black people, he meant that white people have lower time preferences, a farsightedness that allows them to maintain self-discipline and accumulate wealth.[115] Beale contrasts the civilized whites with "the pure savage [who] lives entirely in the moment and does not control his impulses."[116] His argument sounds remarkably like the one presented by Cochran and Harpending, but he just as easily could have drawn upon Hans-Hermann Hoppe's *Democracy—The God That Failed* (2001) or Edward C. Banfield's *The Unheavenly City Revisited* (1974).[117] Reactionary discourse often slanders Black people as impetuous criminals who commit antisocial acts due to their allegedly high time preferences.

Racist pseudoscience has also long held that white people are naturally given to forethought. Madison Grant's *The Passing of the Great Race* (1916) argues that cold winters killed off Northern Europeans who did not have the "industry and foresight [to prepare] the year's food, clothing, and shelter during the short summer," leaving only the provident behind to become the white race.[118] Richard Lynn and J. Phillippe Rushton revived the cold winters hypothesis in almost identical terms in the 1980s and

115. Theodore Beale [Vox Day], "Mailvox: Time-Preferences and Civilization," *Vox Popoli*, June 19, 2013, https://web.archive.org/web/20220816221100/https://voxday.net/2013/06/19/mailvox-time-preferences-and/.

116. Beale, "Mailvox."

117. Hoppe, *Democracy*, 1–6, 67; Edward C. Banfield, *The Unheavenly City Revisited* (Boston: Little, Brown, and Company, 1974), 57–63, 87. On Hoppe, see Quinn Slobodian, "Anti-'68ers and the Racist-Libertarian Alliance: How a Schism among Austrian School Neoliberals Helped Spawn the Alt Right," *Public Culture* 15, no. 3 (2019): 372–86.

118. Madison Grant, *The Passing of the Great Race, or, The Racial Basis of European History* (New York: Charles Scribner's Sons, 1919), 170. See Rieder, Colonialism, 132-3.

1990s, sometimes using it explain the purported high intelligence of Asian as well as white populations.[119]

Beale alludes to Rushton, whose life-history approach argues that race determines temporality.[120] Rushton's work depends on the r/K selection theory proposed by Robert MacArthur and E. O. Wilson. They argue that r-selected species produce large broods that are quickly abandoned to chance, while K-selected species invest more time in a small number of offspring. Rushton illegitimately applies this outdated theory of interspecies difference to racialized groups within the human species: Black people are more r-selected, and white people are more K-selected.[121] He claims that white life histories steadily progress toward ensuring the success of future generations, while Black people live fast and die young, leaving behind many unclaimed children who survive by chance. Although Beale often uses r/K selection as a metaphor rather than a literal scientific concept—he expresses skepticism about evolution—Beale agrees with Rushton's basic ideas about Black life histories.[122] Beale

119. Richard Lynn, "The Intelligence of the Mongoloids: A Psychometric, Evolutionary, and Neurological Theory," *Personality and Individual Differences* 8, no. 6 (1987): 832; Richard Lynn, "The Evolution of Racial Differences in Intelligence," *Mankind Quarterly* 31, no. 1 (Fall 1991): 99–121; J. Philippe Rushton, *Race, Evolution, and Behavior: A Life History Perspective*, 3rd ed. (Port Huron, Mich.: Charles Darwin Research Institute, 2000), 228–30.

120. Camestros Felapton, "Weird Internet Ideas: r/K and the Far Right," November 4, 2017, https://camestrosfelapton.wordpress.com/2017/11/04/weird-internet-ideas-rk-and-the-far-right/.

121. Sussman, *The Myth of Race*, 262–64; Rushton, *Race, Evolution, and Behavior*, 199–213.

122. Theodore Beale [Vox Day], "Mailvox: Evolutionary Ideology," *Vox Popoli*, May 5, 2012, https://web.archive.org/web/20240503004208/https://voxday.net/2012/05/05/mailvox-evolutionary-ideology/; Theodore Beale [Vox Day], "Mailvox: Clinging to the Myth," *Vox Popoli*, December 29, 2013, https://web.archive.org/web/20240503004155/https://voxday.net/2013/12/29/mailvox-clinging-to-my/.

would later embrace the alt-right and endorse a version of David Lane's white supremacist Fourteen Words slogan.[123]

Now that we have unpacked Beale's vituperations against Jemisin, it becomes clear that the inciting event for the Rabid Puppies movement rested on a fundamental conflict over the racial nature of time. Beale attacked Jemisin because he believed that as a future-oriented genre science fiction is inherently white and closed to Black people. Jemisin proved him wrong by launching one of the most illustrious careers in postmillennial speculative fiction, but these ideas persist throughout the far right. The Rabid Puppies scandal turned out to be rooted in a battle over who has the capacity to imagine the future.

Ostracized by most of science fiction fandom for his racist trolling, Beale saw the Rabid Puppies as an opportunity to wreak vengeance on the field. In terms of literary content, both the Sad Puppies and Rabid Puppies campaigns seemed backward looking. The Sad Puppies called for a return to the Campbell years of science fiction, while the Rabid Puppies militated for a renewal of pulp fiction along the lines of Edgar Rice Burroughs and Robert E. Howard.[124]

But Beale's public persona during these affairs privileges his relationship to futurity. Beale often wrote from the perspective of a criminal mastermind who, like Doctor Doom or a James Bond villain, seemed to possess ingenious planning capabilities.[125] Everything in the campaign supposedly followed his cunning plans in which every possible outcome—including apparent defeat—was a victory already foreseen.[126]

123. Theodore Beale [Vox Day], "What the Alt-Right Is," *Vox Popoli*, August 24, 2016, https://web.archive.org/web/20231211034735/https://voxday.net/2016/08/24/what-alt-right-is/.

124. Felapton, *Debarkle*, 389.

125. Felapton, 267.

126. Theodore Beale [Vox Day], "Xanatos Unveiled," *Vox Popoli*, August 1, 2015, https://web.archive.org/web/20240503004843/https://voxday.net/2015/08/01/xanatos-unveiled/.

Historical events seem to have proven otherwise. The Rabid Puppies were shut out, and the Hugo Awards still continue (albeit not without subsequent political controversies).[127] Nevertheless, Beale's failure did not stop him from applying this rhetorical strategy to electoral politics. Beale became wrapped up in QAnon, a conspiracy theory claiming that Donald Trump had orchestrated an immense secret operation to expose and convict all his political enemies as Satan-worshipping pedophiles.[128] Beale condemned Democratic operatives and nonwhite immigrants as heathen cannibals perpetrating child sacrifices, consuming reproductive and civilizational futurity.[129] But he knew Trump would win against them. Even Trump's electoral defeat in 2020 became in Beale's eyes another clever plot by the most brilliant tactician ever, the president he hailed as God-Emperor. "Trust the plan," as the QAnon cultists would say.[130]

"No More Lily-White Futures"

The temporalities we have examined in this chapter are structured by whiteness. White time casts the present as a fleeting transition

127. See Alexandra Alter, "Some Authors Were Left Out of Awards Held in China. Leaked Emails Show Why," *New York Times*, February 17, 2024, https://www.nytimes.com/2024/02/17/books/booksupdate/hugo-awards-china.html.

128. Felapton, *Debarkle*, 375–78.

129. Theodore Beale [Vox Day], "Cannibalism Is a Social Construct," *Vox Popoli*, February 22, 2018, https://web.archive.org/web/20240503004819/https://voxday.net/2018/02/22/cannibalism-is-a-social-construct/; Theodore Beale [Vox Day], "Evil in High Places," *Vox Popoli*, April 12, 2018, https://web.archive.org/web/20221203032531/https://voxday.net/2018/04/12/evil-in-high-places-2/.

130. Theodore Beale [Vox Day], "Trust the President," *Vox Popoli*, November 5, 2015, https://web.archive.org/web/20221007213844/https://voxday.net/2020/11/05/trust-the-president/.

on the way to an anticipated goal.[131] Whiteness therefore demands sacrifice: it denies the body and defers its demands in the service of a long-awaited transcendence that will never come.[132] Some white people double down on this temporality when it disappoints them. Social psychologist Raphael S. Ezekiel's group portrait of white nationalists leading dead-end lives in the 1990s describes them as dwelling in the present: "The piece of time they live in is also small . . . a couple of days at the most. The subject was almost always *now*."[133] Bereft of hope or imagination, inhabiting "a world with no possibilities," white nationalists try to expand the scope of their temporal horizons by embracing the fictive past and confected destiny offered by racist mythology.[134] This aimless despair has become a generalized condition now that late capitalism makes it appear impossible to hope or plan for anything in the long run.[135] Under these social conditions, many white men are left with an impoverished historical consciousness that cannot find any way out of the present except through libertarianism's Horatio Alger fantasies and, when those fail, a chiliastic leap into a perfect white world. White temporality therefore offers a depleted and paralyzing view of the here-and-now, one that fails to see that each moment contains traces of the past with unrealized possibilities as well as nascent prefigurations of dawning futures.[136]

As we have seen, science fiction and other speculative genres have often divided the world into those who have a future and

131. Shannon Winnubst, *Queering Freedom* (Bloomington: Indiana University Press, 2006), 158.

132. Winnubst, 159–60.

133. Raphael S. Ezekiel, *The Racist Mind: Portraits of American Neo-Nazis and Klansmen* (New York: Viking, 1995), 314.

134. Ezekiel, 314.

135. Mathias Nilges, *Right-Wing Culture in Contemporary Capitalism: Regression and Hope in a Time without Future* (New York: Bloomsbury, 2020), 22–29.

136. Ernst Bloch, *Heritage of Our Times,* trans. Neville and Stephen Plaice (Berkeley: University of California Press, 1991), 113.

those who reside in the past or present. These divisions have always been racial and political, frequently placing white producers on the side of tomorrow while banishing everyone else to futureless savagery. Optimistic mutational romances gave way to apocalyptic narratives about makers and takers, but the narrative remains remarkably durable.

Nick Land's fantasies take these ideas to the extreme when he insinuates that nerds are being used as remote manipulators of a Terminator-style artificial intelligence from the future to constitute itself in the present "as if a tendril of tomorrow were burrowing back."[137] Land's irrational contempt for the present leads him from temporal confusion and philosophical incoherence into suicidal ideation. He looks forward to a god-like computer that will initiate a positive feedback loop of self-improving intelligence, assimilating the entire solar system including human biomass. Using atoms for any purposes more short-term than digital immortality appears trivial and futile to him. Indeed, Land denigrates all ends other than the naked pursuit of instrumental reason. He imagines a perfectly roundabout method of production that produces nothing other than more efficient versions of its own means of production, an infinitely self-revolutionizing capital that somehow never realizes itself in consumption.[138] This is time preference zero. Nevertheless, for all his extravagance, Land's dreams of nerd supremacy are only the

137. Nick Land, "Meat," *Fanged Noumena, Collected Writings 1987–2007* (Cambridge, Mass.: Urbanomic, 2011), 415. See Benjamin Noys, *Malign Velocities: Accelerationism and Capitalism* (Winchester, UK: Zero Books, 2014), 54–58; Shuja Haider, "The Darkness at the End of the Tunnel: Artificial Intelligence and Neoreaction," *Viewpoint Magazine*, March 28, 2017, https://viewpointmag.com/2017/03/28/the-darkness-at-the-end-of-the-tunnel-artificial-intelligence-and-neoreaction/; Elizabeth Sandifer, "Neoreaction a Basilisk," in *Neoreaction a Basilisk: Essays on and around the Alt Right*, 5–174 (Monee, Ill.: Eruditorium Press, 2017).

138. Nick Land, "Teleoplexy: Notes on Acceleration," *#Accelerate: The Accelerationist Reader*, eds. Robin Mackay and Armen Avanessian (2014; repr. Cambridge, Mass.: MIT Press, 2017), 511.

latest in a discursive tradition that includes pulp novels, capitalist propaganda, and racist pseudoscience.

Although Land remains a marginal character even on the right, we see echoes of this ideology throughout Silicon Valley culture. A new generation of geeks has embraced longtermism, the belief that we should prioritize the well-being of the trillions unborn who may someday exist in the distant future. As part of the project, some right-wing longtermists lobby for pronatalist practices and policies that ensure that the future will be populated by the descendants of the most intelligent and productive citizens.[139] Several longtermist thinkers worry that geniuses may be outbred by the intellectually stunted, who will halt technological progress by bringing about *Idiocracy*.[140] To reverse this trend, some longtermists hope to emulate Genghis Khan by producing enough offspring that they'll eventually constitute a major planetary population.[141] These plans are no longer purely speculative: tech entrepreneurs such as Peter Thiel are investing in reproductive technologies to make this happen.[142] By generating a super race of "Gattaca babies" that'll someday rule the world, these right-wing geeks intend to "set the future of our

139. Julia Black, "Billionaires Like Elon Musk Want to Save Civilization by Having Tons of Genetically Superior Kids. Inside the Movement to Take 'Control of Human Evolution,'" *Business Insider,* November 17, 2022, https://www.businessinsider.com/pronatalism-elon -musk-simone-malcolm-collins-underpopulation-breeding-tech-2022-11.

140. Nick Bostrom, "Existential Risks: Analyzing Human Extinction Scenarios and Related Hazards," *Journal of Evolution and Technology* 9, March 2002, https://www.jetpress.org/volume9/risks.html; William MacAskill, *What We Owe the Future* (New York: Basic Books, 2022), 156; Émil P. Torres, "Understanding 'Longtermism': Why This Suddenly Influential Ideology Is So Toxic," *Salon,* August 20, 2022, https://www .salon.com/2022/08/20/understanding-longtermism-why-this-suddenly -influential-philosophy-is-so/.

141. Julia Black, "Billionaires Like Elon Musk."

142. Black.

species."[143] All of this sounds even more sinister when we realize that longtermism has always been racialized.

Coda: Nazi Ufology

In this chapter, we have seen how many authors use science fiction to figure white people as taking the next step in evolution, but some fascists believe these stories about mutants and aliens to be literally true. They argue that white people descend from a superpowered race of extraterrestrials or god-men.[144] Many ufologists starting in the 1950s adopted the racist ideas of George Hunt Williamson, a disciple of fascist leader William Dudley Pelley, who imagined an advanced race of Nordic aliens locked in a cosmic battle against a conspiracy of small, sickly aliens with "oriental type eyes" who manipulate others for materialistic gain.[145] The gray alien of popular imagination thus emerged out of antisemitic stereotype. While alien researchers wrote about blond-haired, blue-eyed extraterrestrials, occult fascists claimed that flying saucers were piloted by a break-away group of Nazis who established secret bases in Antarctica, the hollow earth, or another dimension after their apparent defeat in the Second World War.[146]

AltRight Corporation cofounder Jason Reza Jorjani takes up all of this in his own white supremacist writings, especially in his didactic science fiction novel *Faustian Futurist* (2020) and his New Age opus

143. Malcolm Collins qtd in Julia Black, "Billionaires Like Elon Musk."
144. Nicholas Goodrick-Clarke, *The Occult Roots of Nazism: Secret Aryan Cults and Their Influence on Nazi Ideology* (New York: New York University Press, 2004), 94–97, 167–68.
145. George Hunt Williamson qtd in Christopher F. Roth, "Ufology as Anthropology: Race, Extraterrestrials, and the Occult," in *E.T. Culture: Anthropology in Outerspaces,* ed. Debbora Battaglia (Durham, N.C.: Duke University Press, 2005), 56–57.
146. Nicholas Goodrick-Clarke, *Black Sun: Aryan Cults, Esoteric Nazism and the Politics of Identity* (New York: New York University Press, 2002), 160–62, 189.

Closer Encounters (2021).[147] Jorjani is an Iranian-American who claims that the Persian race will someday return to its former Aryan glory once advanced genetic manipulation removes the Arabic and Mongol admixtures from the population's genomes.[148] Alluding to Williamson, Pelley, and Nazi UFO mythology, Jorjani argues that postwar Nazis fled the allies by time traveling to the distant past where they established civilizations on Mars, the moon, and the lost continent of Atlantis. Using eugenics, they evolved into a race of Nordic supermen who ruled as gods on antediluvian earth, engineering humankind to serve as slaves divided by racial castes. In a scenario that recalls the time travel paradoxes of science fiction, Jorjani speculates that the Nordics may have interbred with Cro-Magnons to produce the white race with its purportedly unique genetic gifts.[149] The Nordic invaders from the future now plan "their reemergence with the patience of titans, each of whose lives span thousands of years, and who have total recall from one incarnation to the next."[150]

However, the Atlanteans and their descendants are divided into two factions. The Olympian traditionalists want to close the loop of cyclical time by recreating a static totalitarian order, but they are opposed by the Promethean or Faustian futurists, fascists who want to break into an open-ended future.[151] The anti-Olympian resistance is aided by an even more superior entity from millions of years hence who has traveled to our present era in order to "ex-

147. See Harrison Fluss and Landon Frim, "Aliens, Antisemitism, and Academia," *Jacobin,* March 11, 2017, https://jacobin.com/2017/03/jason-reza -jorjani-stony-brook-alt-right-arktos-continental-philosophy-modernity -enlightenment.

148. Carol Schaeffer, "Alt Fight," *The Intercept,* March 18, 2018, https:// theintercept.com/2018/03/18/alt-right-jason-jorjani/.

149. Jason Reza Jorjani, *Closer Encounters* (London: Arktos, 2021), 179. Kindle.

150. Jason Reza Jorjani, *Faustian Futurist* (London, Arktos, 2020), 68.

151. Jorjani, *Closer Encounters,* 12, 301, 312.

pand the existential horizon of possibilities for life at any cost."[152] The Prometheans intend to achieve this expansion by using their exceptional "foresight"—"the superior power of precognition, projection, and anticipation"—to overthrow the Olympian gods and bring about a technoscientific revolution.[153]

Jorjani sides with the Faustian rebels, but that insurrectionary impulse shouldn't be taken as a wholesale rejection of his former alt-right comrades. Jorjani believes that the Faustian spirit is unevenly distributed: "Only a small minority of individuals, comparable to Magneto's band of rebel mutants, will be strong enough to take the leap into a positively Posthuman future."[154] The Olympians want to rule over baseline humans, but the Faustians remain indifferent to them. Jorjani is evasive on this count, but he indicates many people will die in the upheaval leading up to the Faustian ascendence, including large numbers of Muslims and others he believes to be unfit to be free. Jorjani's heroes follow in the footsteps of not only X-Men's Brotherhood of Evil Mutants but also Mary Shelley's Frankenstein, Star Trek's Khan, the Incredible Hulk, and the Ghostbusters in risking baseline humanity's total destruction in the pursuit of Promethean fire.[155]

Steeped in scientific racism, Jorjani seems to believe that Faustian mutants will generally be found in the white population. He argues that Indo-Europeans are responsible for most discovery and exploration, because only "Western man is ceaselessly driven beyond himself, as restless as a vampire in the night of time."[156] Jorjani alleges that Chinese people demonstrate a "fear of change"

152. Emphasis removed. Jason Reza Jorjani, *Closer Encounters* (London: Arktos, 2021), 12.

153. Jason Reza Jorjani, "Towards a Prometheist Platform," *Prometheism*, January 14, 2021, https://web.archive.org /web/20210118025811/https://prometheism.com/about/f/towards-a -prometheist-platform.

154. Jason Reza Jorjani, *Prometheism* (London: Arktos, 2020), xxv.

155. Jorjani, *Prometheism*, 60, 224–32.

156. Jorjani, *Faustian*, 81.

and Africans have "poor impulse control," while Arabs and "the Dravidian majority in India" betray an "undisciplined and unfocused laziness."[157] White people, Jorjani claims, possess "the genetic predisposition to bold inquisitiveness, curiosity to the point of dangerous risk taking, iconoclastic individuality, wondrous enjoyment of pure creativity, and a horizon-expanding will to transcend all apparent limitations."[158] Jorjani provides a precise description of the Faustian myth, which we will examine in the next chapter.

157. Jorjani.
158. Jorjani.

2. Whitey on the Moon

RICHARD SPENCER MAY BE one of the most significant unrecognized science fiction critics of our time. On his podcasts, he has devoted dozens of discussions to critiquing science fiction films and novels ranging from the *Star Wars* franchise to Stanley Kubrick's *2001: A Space Odyssey* and *A Clockwork Orange*. Spencer is drawn to science fiction because he believes that speculative scenarios sneak illiberal ideas past gatekeepers who would otherwise balk at them if they were presented in realist narratives. Speculation motivates Spencer's politics, as well. At the height of his notoriety Spencer promoted a science fiction vision of the future, telling mainstream journalists that only white people possess what he calls a "a Faustian drive or spirit—a drive to explore, a drive to dominate, a drive to live one's life dangerously . . . a drive to explore outer space and the universe."[1] Most people think of the far right as offering stability and permanence in an increasingly chaotic world, but Spencer's project is to convince European civilization to recover this "desire for exploration, for risk-taking, for shooting the stars."[2] Spencer

1. Richard Spencer, qtd in Josh Harkinson, "Meet the White Nationalist Trying to Ride the Trump Train to Lasting Power," *Mother Jones*, October 27, 2016, https://www.motherjones.com/politics/2016/10/richard-spencer-trump-alt-right-white-nationalist/.

2. Richard Spencer, qtd in George Hawley, *Making Sense of the Alt-Right* (New York: Columbia University Press, 2017), 65.

therefore turns to what he calls "Faustian science fiction" to remind white people of their true nature, which he insists is bound up in an urge to expand outward past all frontiers even if that means dying tragically while doing so.[3]

Spencer expounded upon this idea at length in an early podcast that explicated Christopher Nolan's *Interstellar* (2014) with alt-right essayist Roman Bernard. *Interstellar* caused a big stir among alt-right intellectuals because it expressed the widespread reactionary sentiment that the United States had undergone a serious social and technological decline. The country's malaise, they suggested, could only be reversed by intrepid white explorers taking up where the Apollo missions left off. In the film, the United States has shifted all resources away from technological innovation and into food production after an environmental catastrophe reduces the planet to a dustbowl. Even as the government denies the possibility of spaceflight—they claim the moon landing was an expensive hoax—a secret NASA program strives to save humanity by sending settlers to colonize another planet.

The film captures Spencer's imagination with the image of Joseph Cooper, a salt-of-the-earth farmer venturing into the cosmos to preserve his bloodline descendants. When the mission goes awry, Cooper gambles his life on diving into a black hole to obtain the antigravity formula that will allow his children to escape from a dying earth onto orbital colonies. Somehow, entering the black hole's singularity allows Cooper to transmit the formula back in time. Spencer likens him to the Terminator, a powerful visitor from the future revising the past.[4]

According to Spencer, Cooper embodies the settler-colonial spirit that motivated the Columbus expedition and the Mayflower voyage, an Aryan élan that is now sorely lacking. Both Spencer and Bernard

3. Richard Spencer, interview with Roman Bernard, "Faustian Identity," *Radix*, podcast audio, November 14, 2014, author's archive.
4. Richard Spencer and Mark Brahmin, "Unconscious Cinema—The Terminator," *Radix*, podcast audio, August 9, 2017, author's archive.

agree that NASA's "Faustian ambitions" represented by Cooper have been smothered by a ruling class of "human resource managers," who are more interested "raising the self-esteem of Muslims or fulfilling diversity quotas" than launching piloted space missions.[5]

The alt-right frequently blames multiculturalism for spaceflight's stagnation. In his 2016 book *"Whitey on the Moon": Race, Politics, and the Death of the U.S. Space Program, 1958–1972,* racist blogger Michael J. Thompson (writing as Paul Kersey) suggests that *Interstellar* is a wake-up call for white people.[6] He complains that the nation was promised space travel but got a deindustrialized Detroit. Thompson attacks lawmakers for listening to the scathing poem "Whitey on the Moon" by Gil Scott-Heron, who contrasted the well-funded moon mission with the misery of Black workers in decaying slums.[7] According to Thompson, money spent on welfare payments to Black people could have been allocated to fund crewed missions to Mars.[8] His screed singles out Nichelle Nichols, the Black actor who played Lt. Nyota Uhura in *Star Trek,* because she helped NASA recruit nonwhite personnel. Kersey's false revisionist history depicts spaceflight as a uniquely white achievement that was undermined by NASA's racial integration in the 1970s.

Thompson's book ignores both the important role played by Black women mathematicians at NASA as well as the racial discrimination that persisted in the program long after lunar missions ceased.[9]

5. Spencer, "Faustian Identity."

6. Jared Holt, "Hiding in Plain Sight: The White Nationalist Who Toiled Inside a Right-Wing Media Powerhouse," *Right Wing Watch,* February 3, 2020, https://www.rightwingwatch.org/post/hiding-in-plain -sight-the-white-nationalist-who-toiled-inside-a-right-wing-media -powerhouse/.

7. See Neil M. Maher, *Apollo in the Age of Aquarius* (Cambridge, Mass.: Harvard University Press, 2017), 11–14, 20–53.

8. See Patricia Ventura and Edward K. Chan, *White Power and American Neoliberal Culture* (Oakland, Calif.: University of California Press, 2023), 92.

9. Margot Lee Shetterly, *Hidden Figures: The American Dream and the Untold Story of the Black Women Mathematicians Who Helped Win the Space*

NASA—which was never all-white—did not undergo a radical shift in racial composition after Apollo. An outraged Thompson later twisted himself into a pretzel trying to discredit *Hidden Figures* (2016), the film that popularized the accomplishments of Black employees such as Katherine Johnson at NASA and its predecessor NACA during the space race.[10] All his arguments overlook the real causes for the program's fate: neoliberal legislators took advantage of dwindling support for NASA following the space race's conclusion to slash its budget while redirecting funds to earthside military technologies.[11]

Nevertheless, Thompson targets Nichols for supposedly ruining NASA because she represents the "racial utopia" that white nationalism opposes.[12] Lt. Uhura along with George Takei's Lt. Hikaru Sulu offered nonwhite audiences a glimpse into an antiracist future, appearing on the starship's deck as equals to white crew members.[13] Uhura even inspired the first Black woman astronaut in space, Dr. Mae C. Jemison. Many other alt-right commentators hate *Star Trek* for precisely this reason. Spencer highlights the show's Jewish influences while complaining that the "humans aboard the

Race (New York: William Morrow, 2016); Fred Scharmen, *Space Forces: A Critical History of Life in Outer Space* (New York: Verso, 2021), 161, 166–70.

10. Greg Johnson and Paul Kersey [Michael J. Thompson], "Aryan Dreams Deferred," *Counter-Currents Radio*, February 23, 2017, https://web .archive.org/web/20230604115154/https://counter-currents.com/2017/02 /space-a-dream-deferred/.

11. Scharmen, *Space Forces*, 183–84; David Graeber, "Of Flying Cars and the Declining Rate of Profit," *The Baffler* 19 (March 2012), https:// thebaffler.com/salvos/of-flying-cars-and-the-declining-rate-of-profit.

12. Paul Kersey [Michael J. Thompson], *"Whitey on the Moon": Race, Politics, and the Death of the U.S. Space Program, 1958–1972* (n.p.: SBPDL, 2016), 30.

13. De Witt Douglas Kilgore, *Astrofuturism: Science, Race, and Visions of Utopia in Space* (Philadelphia: University of Philadelphia Press, 2003), 21–28; andré m. carrington, *Speculative Blackness: The Future of Race in Science Fiction* (Minneapolis: University of Minnesota Press, 2016), 68–88.

Enterprise have no sense of ethno-cultural identity whatsoever."[14] Similarly, Greg Johnson argues that the show's multiculturalism contradicts its Faustian spirit of technoscientific discovery because "Faustianism is primarily a white thing."[15] The alt-right sees a multiracial society as antithetical to space exploration.

This is why antifascist science fiction has often been so intertwined with Afrofuturism. Terry Bisson fought fascists as a member of the John Brown Anti-Klan Committee before writing *Fire on the Mountain* (1988), an alternative history in which John Brown's successful rebellion paves the way for an antiracist socialist utopia that sends a Black cosmonaut to Mars.[16] Octavia Butler's dystopian novel *Parable of the Talents* (1998) counterposes Christian nationalist demagogue Andrew Steele Jarret with a Black prophet who dreams of shepherding her multiracial community into interstellar space. The image of a Black person among the stars represents a direct affront to the white-supremacist imaginary.

Nevertheless, reclaiming American supremacy in space has long been a project of the right. Larry Niven and Jerry Pournelle led a council of science fiction authors and technology experts to push for Ronald Reagan's Strategic Defense Initiative, better known as Star Wars.[17] Donald Trump inaugurated the U.S. Space Force at Newt Gingrich's urging, and the seal he approved looked suspiciously like

14. Richard Spencer, "Star Trek and the Jews," *Taki's Magazine*, May 22, 2009, https://web.archive.org/web/20230330143849/https://www.takimag.com/article/sniperstower/star_trek_and_the_jews/.

15. Trevor Lynch [Greg Johnson], "*Star Trek: Beyond*," *Counter-Currents*, August 24, 2016, https://web.archive.org/web/20231205011550/https://counter-currents.com/2016/08/star-trek-beyond/.

16. Hilary Moore and James Tracy, *No Fascist USA! John Brown's Anti-Klan Committee and Lessons for Today's Movement* (San Francisco: City Lights, 2020), 141, 189.

17. Chad Andrews, "Technomilitary Fantasy in the 1980s: Military Sf, David Drake, and the Discourse of Instrumentality," *Extrapolation* 56, no. 2 (2015): 140–42; David Forbes, *The Old Iron Dream* (Oakland, Calif.: Inkshares, 2014).

the emblem for Starfleet Command.[18] NASA elegies have spread beyond the alt-right blogosphere, as well. Tech entrepreneur and far-right patron Peter Thiel complained "we wanted flying cars, instead we got 140 characters," a theme he would take up again in his keynote address to the inaugural National Conservativism Conference in 2019, where he expressed disappointment that we have developed the *"Star Trek* computer" but we had not invented other *Star Trek* technology such as the warp drive or replicators.[19] Similarly, conservative columnist Ross Douthat compares midcentury science fiction's optimistic predictions with what he sees as the decades of decline following the triumphant Apollo lunar mission.[20] They claim our hope for a spacefaring future is predicated on a strong, right-wing government.

Bernard and Spencer indict egalitarian gender politics for dooming spaceflight, as well. They claim that liberals subordinated Faustian culture to the feminizing ideal of security. Now that the frontiers have been closed, nothing remains beyond what Bernard calls the "prison-supermarket," a commercialized world that has left many white men "boring, fat, emasculated, and actually not really human."[21] They have become like Nietzsche's Last Man, a spent figure with no ambitions beyond the present moment's short-lived

18. Vanessa Romo, "Trump Unveils New Space Force Logo, Inciting 'Star Trek' Fan Outrage," *NPR,* January 24, 2020, https://www.npr.org/2020 /01/24/799396583/trump-unveils-new-space-force-logo-inciting-star-trek -fan-outrage.

19. Peter Thiel, qtd in Max Chafkin, *The Contrarian: Peter Thiel and Silicon Valley's Pursuit of Power* (New York: Penguin Books, 2021), 163. National Conservatism, "Peter Thiel: The Star Trek Computer Is Not Enough—National Conservatism Conference," *YouTube,* 40:05, July 16, 2019, https://www.youtube.com/watch?v=7JRyy2MM-rI&ab_channel= NationalConservatism.

20. Ross Douthat, *The Decadent Society: How We Became the Victims of Our Own Success* (New York: Avid Reader Press, 2020), 1–6, 210–15, 234–40.

21. Bernard, "Faustian Identity."

satisfactions.[22] Supposedly, only a hardened masculinity now lost can endure hardship to reach for the stars.

Bernard proposes an alternative genre politics for the alt-right when he asserts, "We are not hobbits!"[23] In J. R. R. Tolkien's fiction, the hobbits are parochial and complacent conservatives who only want to remain in their burrows free from outside influence. These furry-footed creatures were later taken up as mascots by Italian neo-fascists, who in the 1970s organized Hobbit Camps to appeal to white youth sympathetic to right-wing traditionalism and back-to-nature themes.[24] Campers included the future Italian Prime Minister Giorgia Meloni.[25] Hobbits also appealed to Steve Bannon, who used the term with approval to describe antiglobalists among working-class middle Americans.[26] However, although Spencer and Bernard agree on the importance of finding roots in one's homeland, they reject any form of localism or traditionalism that would prevent Aryans from leaving this planet. They insist that attachment to place is an Indigenous rather than European trait.

For similar reasons, Spencer opposes the "bad ethnostate" that he sees in *Elysium* (2013), a science fiction film in which the wealthy leave the poor behind to live on a ring-shaped rotating space habitat.[27] Many on the far right decried the film as an "open borders propaganda farce" in which a white protagonist sacrifices himself to destroy the "white enclave" in space by granting entry and citi-

22. See Michael O'Meara, *New Culture, New Right: Anti-Liberalism in Postmodern Europe* (London: Arktos, 2013), 34.

23. Bernard, "Faustian Identity."

24. Roger Griffin, "Revolts against the Modern: The Blend of Literary and Historical Fantasy in the Italian New Right," *Literature & History* 11, no. 1 (2002): 103.

25. Jason Horowitz, "Hobbits and the Hard Right: How Fantasy Inspires Italy's Potential New Leader," *New York Times*, September 21, 2022, https://www.nytimes.com/2022/09/21/world/europe/giorgia-meloni-lord-of-the-rings.html.

26. Benjamin R. Teitelbaum, *War for Eternity: Inside Bannon's Far-Right Circle of Global Power Brokers* (New York: Dey Street Books, 2020), 74.

27. Spencer, "Faustian Identity."

zenship to nonwhite immigrants from Earth.[28] But Spencer thinks the Elysium space station is not worth saving. Spencer has always distinguished himself from other white nationalists by arguing that white people should rule over the world rather than exit into secessionist fortresses. He likens Elysium to the traditional conservative vision of returning to the year 1955 by retreating into gated suburbs. This rearguard action betrays what he believes to be the inherent expansionism of the white identity, which demands a restless and risky pursuit of the beyond. Rallying the fascist geeks, Spencer responds, "We need identitarianism in space . . . Our identity is to die exploring the moons of Jupiter."[29]

Because they see technoscientific exploration as an expression of white Faustian identity, white nationalists incorrectly attribute deindustrialization and the concomitant technological slowdown to gender and racial chaos. Marshall Berman offers a better way to understand modernity's Faustian character: Goethe's sorcerer represents a figure for the capitalist developmental drive, which runs roughshod over traditional constraints as it revolutionizes itself in the pursuit of infinite growth.[30] However, as Moishe Postone points out, fascists have long misrecognized capitalism's dynamic tendencies as expressions of the Aryan race's biological imperative to expand and dominate.[31] They believe economic prosperity is driven by white population increase and territorial enlargement. Because the far right posits white demographic decline as the un-

28. Matthew Heimbach, "*Elysium* Is an Anti-White Open Borders Farce," *Traditionalist Youth Network,* August 20, 2013, http://web.archive .org/web/20170816050632/http://www.tradyouth.org/2013/08/elysium-is -an-anti-white-open-borders-propaganda-farce/.

29. Spencer, "Faustian Identity."

30. Marshall Berman, *All That Is Solid Melts into Air: The Experience of Modernity* (New York: Penguin, 1988), 39–41.

31. Moishe Postone, "Anti-Semitism and National Socialism: Notes on the German Reaction to 'Holocaust,'" *New German Critique* 19, special issue 1: "Germans and Jews" (Winter 1980): 110.

derlying cause of capitalism's long downturn, they maintain that ethnic cleansing is the only way to bring back the boom times.[32]

But capitalism's inner contradictions are the real cause of the current stagnation. As the rate of profit declines, private firms no longer invest at high levels in technologies that might dramatically increase productivity growth and improve everyday life.[33] Research and development spending falls while capital, technical personnel, and other resources are diverted into socially negligible pursuits governed by short-term financial interests such as stock buybacks or targeted advertising. The alt-right's race thinking proves to be a major impediment to imagining what would be required for a genuine break with the present social and technological stasis.

God Emperor

Spencer explores the notion of Faustian science fiction in another podcast with Counter-Currents publisher Greg Johnson and Arktos Media publisher John Morgan, two leading figures in the white nationalist public sphere. The podcast focused on Frank Herbert's *Dune* (1965), a popular science fiction novel among fascists.[34] Set on an arid planet in the far future, the novel depicts the rise of Paul Atreides after his father is killed by a rival aristocratic family. Cast into the wilderness, Paul inspires the desert peoples to revolt against his enemies, and his triumph brings about his ascension to the position of Emperor. Along the way, Paul develops preternatural prescience, leading his followers to revere him as a

32. Dan Sinykin, *American Literature and the Long Downturn: Neoliberal Apocalypse* (Oxford: Oxford University Press, 2020), 57–58.

33. Jason E. Smith, *Smart Machines and Service Work: Automation in an Age of Stagnation* (London: Reaktion Books, 2020), 95; Aaron Benanav, *Automation and the Future of Work* (New York: Verso, 2020), 42.

34. Jordan S. Carroll, "Race Consciousness: Fascism and Frank Herbert's 'Dune,'" *Los Angeles Review of Books,* November 19, 2020, https://lareviewofbooks.org/article/race-consciousness-fascism-and-frank-herberts-dune/.

messiah. By the second book in the series, Paul has achieved his apotheosis as a god ruling over his empire.

The right-wing podcasters embrace *Dune* because Herbert's universe combines feudal social forms with high technology. Despite the mixture of traditions, religions, and languages seen in the novel, which draws inspiration from Arab and Islamic cultures, Johnson claims *Dune*'s world is spiritually if not genetically European. He argues that *Dune* rejects "*Star Trek* liberalism" in favor of an "updated feudalism."[35] The vast timescales required for space travel, Johnson asserts, require an all-powerful sovereign to keep interstellar voyagers on mission. Hitting on a theme explored in the previous chapter, Johnson maintains that only an antiliberal and antidemocratic government can suppress the fickle demands of the masses—who cannot see past their immediate desires—and impose instead the rule of "people who think and plan over great, long spans of time."[36] But Johnson worries that white people will never conquer "the final frontier" or realize their "Faustian aspirations" because "all of our resources are going to providing cell phones and vaccinations for Epsilon semi-morons," the lowest worker classification in Aldous Huxley's *Brave New World*.[37] Johnson suggests that space exploration will be an elite endeavor organized by an authoritarian dictatorship and funded thanks to austerity programs—or it will not happen at all.

It is easy to see why Paul appeals to Johnson and the rest of the alt-right. Paul refuses to submit to popular demands: as Emperor, he sacrifices sixty billion people in his plan to remake the galaxy and bring its inhabitants under his absolute command. But Herbert

35. Richard Spencer, interview with Greg Johnson and John Morgan, "Archeo-Futurist Messiah," *Radix*, podcast audio, August 14, 2014, https://archive.org/details/soundcloud-207417964.

36. Spencer, interview. See Alexandra Minna Stern, *The Proud Boys and the White Ethnostate: How the Alt-Right Is Warping the American Imagination* (Boston: Beacon Press, 2019), 44–45; Thomas J. Main, *The Rise of the Alt-Right* (Washington, D.C.: Brookings Institution Press, 2018), 147.

37. Spencer, "Archeo-Futurist Messiah."

intended the novel to be a critique of the authoritarianism inherent in the superman figure idolized in *Astounding Science Fiction* under John W. Campbell Jr.'s editorship.[38] The reader is seduced into rooting for Paul in his quest to overthrow the oppressive reign of the Harkonnens only to realize along with him that the path to power has transformed him and later his heir into monsters. Our desire for science fiction saviors, Herbert suggests, leads straight to totalitarianism. Once again, the alt-right ignores irony, parody, or immanent critique in science fiction texts. Through a kind of hermeneutics of obtuseness, alt-right critics wrest right-wing meanings from ostensibly antifascist texts.

Despite its creator's intentions, *Dune* contributes to a fascist discourse on time. Paul achieves his god-like station through the innate foresight that alt-right intellectuals such as Johnson admire. Paul is the product of a generations-long eugenics breeding program by the Bene Gesserit to produce a superhuman being with precognitive psychic abilities. At the start of the novel, Paul undergoes one of the tests used in this program. A Bene Gesserit compels him to place his hand inside a box that produces a painful but harmless sensation; he is instructed that if he removes his hand, he'll be killed with a poisoned needle, the Gom Jabbar. This ordeal serves as a fatal marshmallow test, measuring his ability to deny his immediate impulses and focus instead on the future.[39] The Bene Gesserit claim the test is used to determine if someone is human: only animals live for the present moment. Paul passes, proving that like his ancestors he possesses the discipline and rational awareness to think ahead.

Paul's heritage—along with his consumption of the spice melange—allows him to perceive every possible future. As Joshua Pearson has shown, Paul's ability to navigate the timestreams transforms him into an expert in a risk management that is coded as

38. Frank Herbert, "Dune Genesis," *Omni* 2, no. 10, July 1980: 72.

39. See Michael E. Staub, "Controlling Ourselves: Emotional Intelligence, the Marshmallow Test, and the Inheritance of Race," *American Studies* 55, no. 1 (2016): 69–73.

heroic and masculine.[40] His prescience makes him sensitive to new opportunities and adaptive to circumstances.[41] Spencer admires this quality in Paul, likening his nimble negotiation of catastrophic risk to surfing the deluge.[42] He imagines white people as uniquely suited to handling Black Swan events.

Ultimately, Paul loses himself as he ranges through potential futures, becoming an increasingly alien being estranged from present moment. Although Paul's sacrifice appears tragic to most audiences, his alt-right readers demand a ruler eager to relinquish everything to obtain power. Spencer and Johnson agree that the novel sets up a Hegelian master–slave dialectic wherein Paul proves his mastery through his willingness to risk not only his own death but the destruction of the spice melange, which provides the basis for the known universe's entire civilization. "The power to destroy a thing is the power to control a thing," Spencer intones.[43] Here Spencer and Johnson betray the influence of Ricardo Duchesne, the Arktos author who draws upon Alexandre Kojève's interpretation of Hegel to argue that the Indo-Europeans of the Bronze Age were propelled to greatness by their desire to "fight to the death for pure prestige."[44] This cultural complex supposedly selected for individuals with a genetic propensity toward risk-taking behavior and easily wounded pride, breeding a haughty warrior race inclined to engage in Faustian conquest.[45] Paul's enemies—who fascists equate with Arabs or Jews—are unwilling to play at such high stakes because they are petty misers and debauched decadents

40. Joshua Pearson, "Frank Herbert's *Dune* and the Financialization of Heroic Masculinity," *CR: The New Centennial Review* 19, no. 1 (Spring 2019): 155.

41. Pearson, 171–73.

42. Spencer, "Archeo-Futurist Messiah."

43. Spencer.

44. Alexandre Kojève, qtd in Ricardo Duchesne, *The Uniqueness of Western Civilization* (Leiden: Brill, 2011), 51.

45. Ricardo Duchesne, *Faustian Man in a Multicultural Age* (London: Arktos, 2017).

more interested in hoarding gold than defending honor. Drawing heavily upon antisemitic propaganda, the alt-right readers cast Paul's foes as born slaves. None of these fascists seems to have read far enough in Hegel or Kojève to see that the servant transcends his circumstances through labor, thereby ushering in the future, while the master remains trapped in the transitory pleasures of luxury consumption.[46]

Johnson and Spencer suggest that Paul's refusal to play the game, his unwillingness to compete for spice, makes his ascent to power a genuine rupture with the existing order. The Faustian subject overcomes not only calculable risks but also radical uncertainties. Johnson asserts that the ultimate purpose of Paul's bloodline is to reintroduce contingency and unpredictability into a world increasingly dominated by precognitive systems of control. This falls in line with the dominant reading of the novel, which suggests that Paul is a heroic version of the Mule, the mutant whose surprising novelty disrupts the course planned by the psychohistorians in Isaac Asimov's Foundation trilogy.[47] Later in the *Dune* series, Paul's son God Emperor Leto II undoes his own fascist rule by breeding prophecy-resistant humans and scattering humankind beyond the reach of any other despot who would try to conquer the known universe again. Johnson affirms Leto II's self-overcoming as a Heideggerian event that resists enframing.[48]

At first it seems like Leto II should not fit with the alt-right argument. He improves upon his father's precognition to become "the first truly long-range planner in human history," capable of mapping out millennia, but he sets about deliberately creating an empire so stiflingly totalitarian that it inspires humanity to reject

46. G. W. F. Hegel, *Phenomenology of Spirit,* trans. A. V. Miller (New York: Oxford University Press, 1977), 115–19; Alexandre Kojève, *Introduction to the Reading of Hegel: Lectures on The Phenomenology of Spirit,* trans. James H. Nichols Jr. (Ithaca, N.Y.: Cornell University Press, 1969), 23.

47. Timothy O'Reilly, *Frank Herbert* (New York: Ungar, 1981), 86–87.

48. Spencer, "Archeo-Futurist Messiah."

despotism.[49] Johnson, however, does not see this is a liberal parable. Quite the opposite: he believes Leto II works to ward off the "end of history," the universal triumph of liberal democracy foretold by Francis Fukuyama.[50] Johnson argues that Leto II essentially travesties Fukuyama's vision when he creates a placid society in which an all-women army systematically blocks outlets for white men to exercise their aristocratic self-pride by dominating others, eliminating such competitive pursuits as war, politics, and exploration.[51] In this interpretation, Leto II deliberately generates an explosive psychic pressure that bursts his civilization asunder so as to reopen a "frontier" where this white masculine fighting spirit can finally reassert itself: after thousands of years of "being rapped on the knuckles by burly nuns, patriarchy is going to return with a roar."[52] Never mind that the most prominent rebel against Leto II is a woman: the alt-right insists that white masculine self-expression is the source of all unforeseeable historical change.

By examining these creative misreadings of popular science fiction texts, we begin to see the outlines of what Spencer calls the Faustian. Goethe's Faust wagered his own soul by making a dangerous deal with the devil to acquire knowledge and power before reshaping the world according to his visionary plans. He endured infinite risk to acquire infinite spoils. By the same token, the Faustian in alt-right mythology is a white man whose constitution enjoins him to speculate on the future. Here speculation means both gambling and forecasting: the Faustian subject rises above merely utilitarian concerns by showing his willingness to

49. Frank Herbert, *Children of Dune* (1976; repr. New York: Ace, 2020), 463.

50. Greg Johnson, "The Golden Path: Frank Herbert's *Children of Dune & God Emperor of Dune*," *Counter-Currents*, January 12, 2021, https://web.archive.org/web/20231211121737/https://counter-currents.com/2021/01/the-golden-path/.

51. Johnson, "Golden Path." See Francis Fukuyama, *The End of History and the Last Man* (New York: Free Press, 1992), 181–91.

52. Johnson, "Golden Path."

sacrifice everything that he possesses, including his own life. While bourgeois figures for white mastery might attempt to demonstrate their fitness to rule by prudently governing all those they command, the Faustian proves his aptitude for future greatness by pledging entire populations and planets as collateral. Only one who displays a disregard for the present has access to the future. That is the story they tell themselves, at least.

Reactionary thought has long been enamored with risk-bearing subjects. Eighteenth- and nineteenth-century conservatives claimed that elites were consecrated only after they had faced the perils of combat or commerce.[53] The reactionary rhetoric of risk persists up through the contemporary period. After the 2007–2008 financial crisis, a wave of right-wing populist leaders including Donald Trump, Jair Bolsonaro, and Viktor Orbán embraced a "govern-by-chaos" strategy in which they defied cautious neoliberals and pessimistic progressives by attempting to leverage "radical uncertainty" as an opportunity for gain, all the while offering their precarious followers "symbolic social insurance" that, whatever speculative risks they faced, they could rely on the strength of the sovereign nation.[54] According to the right, power accrues to the ones who hazard the most.

The most extreme discourse on risk, however, arose from the German context. Nietzsche's Zarathustra preached that the self-overcoming master is one who is willing to bet his life on a dice roll for more power.[55] Conservative revolutionary Ernst Jünger warned that bourgeois society was culminating in a universal insurance system designed to equalize risk and compensate for all possible

53. Corey Robin, *The Reactionary Mind*, 2nd ed. (Oxford: Oxford University Press, 2018), 37.

54. Aris Komporozos-Athanasiou, *Speculative Communities: Living with Uncertainty in a Financialized World* (Chicago: University of Chicago, 2022), 97–119.

55. Friedrich Nietzsche, *Thus Spoke Zarathustra: A Book for Everyone and Nobody,* trans. Graham Parkes (Oxford: Oxford University Press, 2005), 99.

injuries.[56] Writing in 1931, he anticipated that this risk regime would give way to an age of insecurity when those who graduated from "the school of danger" in the Great War would hold sway over the meek and indemnified.[57] His prediction soon came true: the Nazi regime put the entire nation at risk in a project that Foucault argues was intended to regenerate the race by "exposing the entire population to universal death."[58]

White Americans also saw risk as a catalyst for their racialization. Theodore Roosevelt's narratives about rugged life at the frontiers of American empire convinced many white male readers that voluntary risk-taking would prevent them from becoming overcivilized. As Jason Puskar puts it, "self-imperilment" came to serve "the broader project of rescuing white men from feminizing racial decadence."[59] Often these imagined flirtations with danger involved antagonistic encounters with racial others who enabled the white risk-taker to rediscover himself and regain his powers through manful struggle.[60]

However, in the alt-right narratives I explore here the Faustian figure is often alone and unmatched. In these cases, risk preserves its educative function because it allows the white subject to wrestle with himself. Racist ideology presents the white man as a disembodied mind or spirit whose ability to rise above the demands of the flesh makes him fundamentally distinct from Black people,

56. Ernst Jünger, "On Danger," *The Weimar Republic Sourcebook*, ed. Anton Kaes, Martin Jay, and Edward Dimendberg (Berkeley: University of California Press, 1994), 370.

57. Jünger, 371.

58. Michel Foucault, *"Society Must Be Defended": Lectures at Collège de France, 1975–1976*, ed. Maurio Bertani and Alessandro Fontana, trans. David Macey (New York: Picador, 2003), 360.

59. Jason Puskar, "'Hazardous Business': Nella Larsen's *Passing* and Risk Racialization," *English Language Notes* 54, no. 2 (Fall/Winter 2016): 100.

60. Toni Morrison, *Playing in the Dark: Whiteness and the Literary Imagination* (New York: Vintage, 1993), 44–53.

who always represent excessive embodiment.[61] Just as self-control allows the white subject to exercise mastery over animal appetites, self-sacrifice allows him to show that he values the ideal over the embodied, the potential over the actual.

Obviously, none of this is true. Alt-right partisans are not the shell-shocked victims of trench warfare. They have led lives of pampered safety made possible by stolen wealth and brutal violence. The most consequential risk-bearing subject on the alt-right is Heather Heyer's murderer, who claims to have felt gravely endangered while driving into a crowd of protesters encased in several tons of steel. Protected by cops, the fascists have very little to fear: they are the ones putting everyone else at risk. Indeed, in some sense white people have always been indemnified. Whatever accidents may befall the insured, racial capitalism guarantees that white supremacy will persist in every possible future.[62]

White nationalism's glorification of risk must therefore be understood not as a genuine openness to radical uncertainty but instead as a predictable example of fascism's aestheticized politics. In fascism, Walter Benjamin tells us, humankind's "self-alienation has reached such a degree that it can experience its own destruction as an aesthetic pleasure of the first order."[63] Death and domination continue, but now totalitarian society sees them all as necessary features of its own artistic expression. The white nationalist shooter is the next step in this process, transforming mass death into mediatized spectacle whose aim is not only racial terror but posthumous ce-

61. Richard Dyer, *White: Essays on Race and Culture* (New York: Routledge, 2017), 39.

62. Ian Baucom, *Specters of the Atlantic: Finance Capital, Slavery, and the Philosophy of History* (Durham, N.C. Duke University Press, 2005), 17; Kara Keeling, *Queer Times, Black Futures* (New York: New York University Press, 2019), 23–29.

63. Walter Benjamin, "The Work of Art in the Age of Mechanical Reproduction," *Illuminations*, trans. Harry Zohn, ed. Hannah Arendt (New York: Schocken, 1968), 241–42.

lebrity. Manosphere misogynist Lyndon McLeod wrote his victims' deaths into his science fiction novels before he murdered them.[64] He recorded a film of himself rehearsing for the killings on an SD card and gave it to his ex-girlfriend, asking her to sell it. Presumably he imagined that the video would increase in value once he had enacted its threat. Whereas the Nazis transformed death into a total artwork, the alt-right circulates it as a speculative commodity that can only be realized if the present relations of brutality continue until tomorrow.

There is therefore nothing genuinely risky about Faustian science fiction. Despite what Johnson claims about the Heideggerian event, the alt-right imagines the future as a continuation of the present. History becomes for them the millennia-long flowering of white identity, one in which all relations of racial domination remain in place, and nothing ever really happens that was not already pre-destined by blood. Fascists imagine that they'll always prevail no matter the danger because of their faith in the limitless possibilities contained within whiteness. What appears to be radical uncertainty turns out to be absolute conviction.

To understand this ideology, we must trace Faustianism's gene-alogy back through Spencer's influences. I will explore Spencer's immediate inspiration in French ethnonationalism before locating the evolution of Faustianism in Oswald Spengler, Francis Parker Yockey, and William Pierce. White nationalists pretend to affirm a radically open future, but Hari Kunzru's 2019 novel *Red Pill* was right when it said that the alt-right's future visions "terrorize us into accepting that this world is inevitable."[65]

64. Marisa Kabas, "His Woman-Hating SciFi Went Viral in the 'Manosphere': If She'd Known, Maybe She Would Have Seen Him Coming," *Rolling Stone,* June 19, 2022, https://www.rollingstone.com/culture/culture-features/denver-shooting-tattoo-alicia-cardenas-lyndon-mcleod-1360771/.

65. Hari Kunzru, *Red Pill* (Knew York: Knopf, 2020), 208.

A White Nationalist Transhumanism

As the podcasters suggest, they see *Dune* and other science fiction texts through the lens of "archeofuturism," a concept formulated by Guillaume Faye.[66] Faye became a strong influence on the far right in the United States after he appeared at the American Renaissance conference and his work was published by Arktos. He started out as a member of Nouvelle Droite or the French New Right, a movement of ethnonationalist intellectuals who rejected egalitarianism while adopting what they saw as Gramscian strategies.[67] The French New Right emerged from Groupement de Recherche et d'Etudes pour la Civilisation Européenne or GRECE, a think tank founded in 1968 with the goal of establishing right-wing hegemony through a project of ideological and cultural subversion through metapolitics.[68]

The French New Right advocated for an "ethnopluralism" in which every race would maintain self-determination by separating into homogeneous states or spheres.[69] Faye broke with GRECE in 1986 and, after a detour into journalism and pornographic film, returned to the political scene in the late 1990s as a man of the most extreme right.[70] Shedding his ideological camouflage, Faye became an unequivocal proponent of white supremacy, which he believed to be threatened by Muslim immigrants.[71] Faye's racism grew more violent over the course of his political career, eventually taking on an overtly exterminationist tone.

Faye expounds upon the political principles of his later period in *Archeofuturism* (1998), a book that sprang out of a science fic-

66. Spencer, "Archeo-Futurist Messiah." See Stern, *Proud Boys and the White Ethnostate,* 44.

67. Stéphane François, "Guillaume Faye and Archeofuturism," in *Key Thinkers of the Radical Right: Behind the Threat to Liberal Democracy,* ed. Mark Sedgwick (New York: Oxford University Press, 2019), 92–93.

68. Tamir Bar-On, *Where Have All The Fascists Gone?* (Burlington, Vt.: Ashgate Publishing Company, 2007), 6–9, 30.

69. Bar-On, 5–6.

70. François, "Guillaume Faye," 93.

71. François, 96–98.

tion story that he came up with as a "gag" on a radio program.[72] Drawing upon misinterpretations of postmodern and poststructuralist thinkers, Faye claimed that the narrative's fanciful neologisms and speculative ideas might reshape politics and, ultimately, civilization itself.[73] Science fiction, he suggested, could write future history. Faye uses this mythmaking to promote archeofuturism, an archaic social order recreated in a world revolutionized by technoscientific innovation. This would be a repetition with a difference—here he cites Nietzsche's eternal return—that would renovate and revive the old values and traditions of the premodern past.[74] Rejecting both linear and cyclical temporalities, Faye likened time to a sphere rolling around on a cloth. The same point might touch the fabric multiple times, but it could be in a different place each time. Through this muddled metaphor borrowed from GRECE cofounder Giorgio Locchi, Faye somehow hoped "to reconcile Evola and Marinetti," the traditionalist and futurist wings of fascism.[75] As in so many science fantasy scenarios, Faye imagines horse-drawn carriages sharing the road with self-driving cars, knights and druids dwelling alongside astronauts and geneticists. According to Faye the distant past and the speculative future could coexist even if Muslim immigrants and native-born Europeans could not.

Archeofuturism holds that each culture's technoscientific development is rooted in its people's *arché* or origin: "The future is not the negation of the tradition and historical memory of a folk, but rather their *metamorphosis,* by which they are ultimately reinforced and regenerated."[76] Alt-right ideologue Michael O'Meara glosses

72. Guillaume Faye, *Archeofuturism: European Visions of the Post-Catastrophic Age,* trans. Sergio Knipe (1998; repr. London: Arktos, 2010), 57.

73. Faye, 53–58.

74. Faye, 74.

75. Faye, 89.

76. Faye, 75. See Roger Griffin, "Foreward: Another Face? Another Mazeway? Reflections on the Newness and Rightness of the European New Right," in Tamir Bar-On, *Where Have All the Fascists Gone?* (Burlington, Vt.: Ashgate Publishing Company, 2007), xiii–xiv.

the archeofuture as a Heideggerian and Nietzschean project of realizing potentials already contained within one's cultural heritage
and actively appropriating authentic traditions in order to make
them new again: "The past in this sense is future, for it functions as
a return backwards, to foundations, where future possibility is rip-
est."[77] Although archeofuturist thinkers reject linear, determinist
conceptions of time as eschatological or mechanistic, their favored
temporality also precludes any real radical rupture with what has
come before. We're supposed to believe that airships, rockets, and
sexy virtual avatars were already somehow hidden within Europe's
primordial destiny. One can see why all of this might be flattering
to Faye's alt-right audience of white, anime-obsessed readers in
the United States.

After laying out his ideas in essay form, Faye's *Archeofuturism* offers us a glimpse of a utopian world that emerges after a catastrophic
race war destroys liberal modernity. European and Slavic peoples
have merged to form a "Eurosiberian Federation" that stands as a
dominant global power.[78] Faye's future is extremely inegalitarian.
The elites are called Faustians: practicing "techno-science as esoteric alchemy," they are the 10–20 percent of the population capable
of heroically enduring the "increased risks, unpredictability and the
opacity of the future."[79] Like their sorcerous antihero namesake,
the Faustian elite engages in dangerous experiments, placing their
very humanity in peril. They modify their own genes and augment
themselves with cyborg technologies. They create "man-animal
hybrids or semi-artificial living creatures" who can be employed
as soldiers or servants, and "decerebrated human clones, which
could be used as organ banks."[80] In one especially grotesque pronatalist fantasy, Faustians generate brainless reproductive organs
pumping out "supersperm," which scientists then use to inseminate

77. O'Meara, *New Culture, New Right,* 162.

78. Faye, *Archeofuturism,* 195.

79. Faye, 168–74.

80. Faye, 85–86.

vat-grown uteruses to increase the white birth rate faster than old-fashioned reproduction would allow.[81]

Faye's science fiction vision places him at odds with many others on the right, who see trans- or posthumanism as a plot to dissolve the identity categories they hold dear. Putin's court philosopher Aleksandr Dugin warns of a future filled with "posthuman" cyborgs and chimeras cut off from the temporal ecstasies of the *Dasein*.[82] American conspiracy theorist Alex Jones does not need Heideggerian jargon to spook his viewers with similar predictions about transgenic gorilla and pig humanoids.[83] Working in a more metaphorical register, Great Replacement theorist Renaud Camus worries that multiculturalism is stripping Europeans of their distinct identities and boiling them down into interchangeable units he likens to the robot from *Metropolis* (1927) or the liquefied-human slurry from *Soylent Green* (1973).[84] Others equate transhumanism with gender nonconformity and sexual deviance. Fascist author Kerry Bolton draws a straight line between the Marquis de Sade's libertine and Donna Haraway's cyborg, arguing that technological progressives seek to create a machine-made being liberated from the constraints of patriarchy, reproductive labor, gender categories, and nature itself.[85]

But Faye is not alone in seeing transhumanism as the next step in Faustian self-transcendence. Even David Duke, the Klansman turned political candidate who made a bid for white nationalism's mainstream acceptance, pontificates about white people cubing

81. Faye, 246.

82. Aleksandr Dugin, *The Fourth Political Theory*, trans. Sergio Knipe (London: Arktos, 2012), 183.

83. "Alex Jones Warns of Pig/Gorilla/Human Hybrids Who Can Talk," *Media Matters,* July 6, 2017, https://www.mediamatters.org/alex-jones/alex-jones-warns-piggorillahuman-hybrids-who-can-talk.

84. Renaud Camus, *You Will Not Replace Us!* (Plieux, France: Chez l'auter), 137–38.

85. Kerry Bolton, *The Perversion of Normality: From the Marquis de Sade to Cyborgs* (London: Arktos, 2021), 493–510.

their IQ scores, moving "beyond man," and exploring the cosmos at faster-than-light speeds: "the universe is constructed so that *anything is possible*."[86] Perhaps this should be unsurprising given transhumanism's historical connection to eugenics.[87] Moreover it shows there is no contradiction between radical genetic manipulation and racial purity in the minds of racists: some seem to think that racial differences will persist no matter how drastically genetic engineering changes humankind.[88]

If Faye's argument sounds like the mutational romances we surveyed last chapter, that is because Faustian science proceeds through speculative storytelling. The Faustian elites set about remaking the planet by implementing *"vast plans* that represent the *anticipated representation of a constructed future."*[89] All of these innovations are prefigured in science fictional visions before they're ever realized: "Aviation, rockets, submarines and nuclear power have sprung from *rationalised fantasies* where the scientific spirit has managed to carry out the plan conceived by the aesthetic."[90] For Faye, fantasy dictates reality, and, indeed, he considers it to be a sign of Europe's deep decay that it cannot produce a science film to rival *Star Wars*.[91] Faye's Faustian elites have developed the technology to colonize Mars and build trains that zip around Earth at 20,000 kilometers per hour not because they're uniquely rational but because they have an unrivaled capacity for imaginative projection.

86. David Duke, *My Awakening* (Covington, La.: Free Speech Press, 1999), 110–11.

87. Alison Bashford, "Julian Huxley's Transhumanism," in *Crafting Humans: From Genesis to Eugenics and Beyond,* ed. Marius Turda (Goettingen: V&R unipress GmbH, 2013), 153–67.

88. Carleton S. Coon, "The Future of the Races of Man," in *Apeman, Spaceman,* ed. Leon E. Stover and Harry Harrison (1968; repr. New York: Berkley Medallion Books, 1970), 150–52.

89. Faye, *Archeofuturism,* 71.

90. Faye, 71.

91. Faye, 101–2.

However, according to Faye most Europeans are incapable of handling the stresses of existential risk and ceaseless change. They are better off shunted into "neo-traditional" agrarian societies where time follows a predictable cycle laid down by nature and custom.[92] Whereas the Faustians inhabit a self-revolutionizing temporality in which nothing remains stable for long, the neo-traditionalists live in the countryside much as their ancestors did in premodern times. In many ways this recalls Nietzsche's argument that only a small group of free spirits have the power to build a new system of cultural orientations for the masses, who have been left "horizonless" by modernity's relentless pursuit of the truth.[93] The hoi polloi enjoy peace of mind even as their eco-friendly lifestyle allows the Faustian elite to consume a disproportionate share of natural resources without endangering the planet. Risk has its rewards.

Faye has less to say about the Muslim immigrants and other people of color who were ethnically cleansed at the founding of the Eurosiberian Federation. When a visitor from the Indian Empire asks what happened to them, the protagonist pauses for a moment before explaining that they were forcibly deported to Madagascar.[94] Nazi official Adolf Eichmann considered this island as an evacuation site for Jews before he oversaw their deportation to concentration camps to be murdered. Whether Faye is engaging in irony or prevarication, his Faustian future expels almost all nonwhite populations from history.

Faustian Antecedents

Faye's archeofuturism resonates with a discourse on Faust that has long pervaded conservative and far-right thought. Faust first

92. Faye, 172–73.

93. Ronald Beiner, *Dangerous Minds: Nietzsche, Heidegger, and the Return of the Far Right* (Philadelphia: University of Pennsylvania Press, 2018), 34–39.

94. Faye, *Archeofuturism*, 224.

became a symbol of Western culture with the publication of *The Decline of the West,* a two-volume work by German conservative Oswald Spengler that appeared in 1918 and 1922. Spengler saw great cultures as organisms with a regular lifecycle of development and decline.[95] Each culture possesses its own destiny, a set of possibilities that it can actualize over the course of its lifespan, and history is nothing more than the fulfillment of these preexisting potentials. During their youth, cultures work out these possibilities through artistic or spiritual expressions, but as they age these potentials become hardened into actualized forms. Then the culture turns outward and enters a civilizational period of materialistic achievement.[96] Despite his protests to the contrary, Spengler was considered a pessimist because he believed the West had already entered its autumn years, predicting that there was nothing left for Europeans to do but stoically accept their remaining life tasks.

Spengler critiques Western culture as Faustian in nature, violating every moral and physical boundary in its quest to explore. The Faustian spirit yearns for the infinite, a desire that manifests itself in the symbol of limitless space.[97] As such the Faustian disdains the proximal realm of bodily experience and anything that can be comprehended by the senses in the present moment. Instead, this restless spirit flees into the outer reaches of abstraction or over the next horizon. Although he ultimately commands the earth, there is something otherworldly about this Faust: only "the Western world-feeling," Spengler suggests, could conceive of "a space of infinite star-systems and distances that far transcends all optical possibilities."[98]

Spengler's *Man and Technics*—a 1931 book reprinted by Arktos—reveals the violence inherent in this Faustian worldview. Spencer

95. Spengler, *The Decline of the West,* 21.
96. Spengler, 31.
97. Spengler, 68, 75–76, 183–84, 278, 334.
98. Spengler, 172.

traces the Faustian urge back to man's nature as a "beast of prey."[99]
While the plant is immobile and the herbivore is evasive, the car-
nivore possesses a ballistic consciousness that perceives targets
from afar and pursues them to the death through the most direct
paths possible.[100] Humans outdo the lion's pounce because they
can improve the techniques that they use to dominate their quarry.
Whereas the nonhuman animal is trapped within "the immediate
here-and-now," the predatory man is a Promethean figure capable
of anticipating future possibilities by developing new technical
means to achieve their ends.[101]

Faustian culture is therefore violent and alienated, approaching
the world as a foe to be subdued and transformed. Spengler claims
that this will-to-power stands as the basis of technological civilization and also as the root of its crisis.[102] While Spengler views the
unfolding of the inner logic of technology as a grim necessity that
Europeans must see through to the end, the author of the preface
to the Arktos edition takes a more affirmative stance to technics,
thrilling at the thought that "through technological extension, the
human hand is today reaching out even beyond the stars, towards
that curtain of radiation which shrouds the mysterious birth of our
universe."[103]

Spengler often talks about humanity in *Man and Technics,* rooting
this narrative in the evolution of the species, but in his formula-
tion only white people can grasp toward deep space or deep time.
Spengler claims that it was a mistake for Europeans spread their
technical knowledge to nonwhite races who do not feel the Faustian
will to technological mastery as an "inner need."[104] Spengler worries

99. Oswald Spengler, *Man and Technics: A Contribution to the
Philosophy of Life,* trans. Charles Francis Atkinson and Michael Putnam
(1931; repr. London: Arktos, 2015), 52.
    100. Spengler, 53–56.
    101. Spengler, 39.
    102. Spengler, 111.
    103. Spengler, 20.
    104. Spengler, 131–32.

that nonwhite people will use what they have learned from the Europeans to destroy industrial civilization, and once they have succeeded in wiping out Faustian culture (i.e., white culture), technological progress will end with machines and skyscrapers abandoned as ruins.

Although Spengler does not rank Europeans as the *only* high culture in history—they were preceded by at least seven others ranging from Chinese to Mesoamerican cultures—he does see them as the only one still making history in the twentieth century. When he turns to "primitive" peoples, he describes them as outside of history, undergoing "the zoological up and down, a planless happening without goal or cadenced march in time."[105] In Spengler's scheme only the Faustians retain a destiny in the current period.

Spengler never fully embraced Nazism, but the Faust legend held a special appeal for many committed Nazis.[106] Alfred Rosenberg's influential antisemitic book *The Myth of the Twentieth Century* (1930) reads Goethe's *Faust* as saying that the Nordic race possesses a "Luciferan" soul that compels it to settle colonial frontiers and invent machine technology purely out of a "bliss in commanding."[107]

Spengler's Faustian myth became a crucial component of white nationalist thought in the United States thanks in large part to Francis Parker Yockey's *Imperium* (1948). Yockey's life reads like a spy thriller. As Matthew Rose suggests, he seemed almost eager to put himself in dangerous situations, which allowed him to test "the purity of his devotion to what he called the Idea, undertaking the lonely sacrifices and voluntary risks he believed its defense required."[108] His extensive ties to authoritarian nationalists

105. Spengler, *Decline of the West,* 167.

106. Inez Hedges, *Framing Faust: Twentieth-Century Cultural Struggles* (Carbondale: Southern Illinois University Press, 2005), 48–51.

107. Alfred Rosenberg, *The Myth of the Twentieth Century: An Evaluation of the Spiritual-Intellectual Confrontations of Our Age,* trans. Vivian Bird (Torrance, Calif.: The Noontide Press, 1982), 157.

108. Matthew Rose, *A World after Liberalism: Philosophers of the Radical Right* (New Haven, Conn.: Yale University Press, 2021), 64.

across the globe led him to crusade for a fascist international, the European Liberation Front.[109]

Although he once maintained a brief connection with anti-Communist senator Joseph McCarthy, Yockey became disillusioned with the United States, and he decided after witnessing the Stalinist purge of so-called cosmopolitan Jews in the 1952 Prague Trials that only the Soviet Union could defend Europe from Jewish-controlled America.[110] Following a series of mysterious journeys around the world that may have even included Cuba and the Soviet Bloc, Yockey was arrested by the FBI when baggage handlers discovered fake identity papers in his suitcase.[111] Long hunted by federal authorities, Yockey killed himself with a potassium cyanide capsule while in custody.[112] Before his suicide, though, he was visited by Willis Carto, an influential far-right antisemite who later published *Imperium* with the Noontide Press and cemented his reputation as not only as a right-wing martyr but also the grand theorist of American racism.

Although Yockey frequently paraphrases and plagiarizes from Spengler, he supplements his work with the ideas of Nazi jurist Carl Schmitt.[113] If Faustian civilization seems to have fallen into a state of decay, this can always be reversed by a man of genius who has the foresight to abandon mechanical notions of causality that assume that the world is governed by stable laws.[114] In this state of emergency, the future leader must grasp that life is exceptional and ever-changing, allowing for dramatic and unprecedented developments that cannot be predicted based on any trendline.[115]

109. Kevin Coogan, *Dreamer of the Day: Francis Parker Yockey and the Postwar Fascist International* (Brooklyn, N.Y.: Autonomedia, 1999), 167–81.

110. Coogan, 238–40, 264–67.

111. Coogan, 20–22.

112. Coogan, 38.

113. Coogan, 74–79.

114. Francis Parker Yockey (Ulrick Varange), *Imperium: The Philosophy of History and Politics* (1948; repr. Sausalito, Calif.: The Noontide Press, 1962), 102–3.

115. Yockey, 13–14.

Only such a sovereign figure—an heir to Hitler, "the hero of the Second World War"—can imagine the radically different future that might await Europeans and their descendants.[116] Resisting the cycle of civilizational decline and initiating a new epoch, he will be what fellow fascists such as Savitri Devi would consider a man "against time."[117]

Yockey's term for his untimely hero archetype is the "Genius," and his "Promethean" role is to realize "the Idea of the Future" by imposing it upon the backwards masses who are always falling behind the times.[118] Without an Idea handed down from above, humans remain like the "primitive" peoples outside of Western culture, locked in an animalistic and ahistorical state concerned only with "economic-reproductive existence," i.e., materialistic gain and carnal pleasure.[119] White men, on the other hand, prove they're worthy of making history by sacrificing their merely animal lives: these "men risk all and die for an Idea."[120] Yockey rejects the United States because he believes its men lost the martial virtue that an Idea demands from its adherents. America has been transformed into a "matriarchy," giving up the adventure of history to live inside "a cocoon-like life within a closed system."[121] The American people embraced their feminine side, pursuing "peace, comfort, security, in short, the values of individual life," a condition that leaves them barred from the future just like Africans and the Sámi.[122] Somehow when Yockey and his followers berate Western man for falling short of Faust they conveniently forget that Goethe's magician spends much of the poem seeking the Eternal Feminine and finally finds peace basking in the glory of the Virgin Mary, Mother of God.

116. Yockey, dedication.

117. Stern, *Proud Boys and the White Ethnostate*, 36–38.

118. Yockey, *Imperium*, 267.

119. Yockey, 43.

120. Yockey, 44.

121. Francis Parker Yockey, *The Enemy of Europe* (York, S.C.: Liberty Bell Publications, 1981), 68

122. Yockey, 69.

According to Yockey, European civilization is prevented from actualizing its full potential by alien "parasites" from other cultures who can never be part of the West's spiritual destiny.[123] Yockey targets Black people and Chinese immigrants, but he singles out Jews especially. According to Yockey, Jews are representatives of the past, remnants of a fossilized civilization that spent its potential over a thousand years ago.[124] This supposedly renders them insensible to anything beyond the dead and calcified reality of actualized forms. As a result of this ontological incapacity, Yockey claims, Jews embrace materialistic philosophies that deny the inner necessity of the Faustian spirit to expand and conquer. Unable to appreciate destiny-thinking, they now strive to pull white people back into the nineteenth century, the century of Marxism and mass democracy. Yockey's race war is a time war between the Jewish past and the white future.[125]

Antisemitism remains at a murderous pitch among white nationalists—in 2018 a gunman affiliated with the alt-right killed eleven people in the Tree of Life synagogue massacre—but as the movement has become increasingly Islamophobic it has transposed Yockey's temporal politics onto Muslims as well. The Proud Boys founder Gavin McInnes told podcast host Joe Rogan that Muslim inbreeding with their first cousins had caused them to go "backwards in time," moving them from the modern to the medieval period, a point that he underscores by making the sound of an audio track running in reverse.[126] McInnes—along with Faye and other anti-Muslim racists—rewrites the clash of civilization narratives as a temporal rift.

If whiteness represents futurity, Yockey asserts his claim on the next century by writing in the future perfect tense. In an almost

123. Yockey, *Imperium,* 376–439.

124. Yockey, 383, 395–96.

125. Yockey, 115–17.

126. Joe Rogan, interview with Gavin McInnes, *The Joe Rogan Experience*, 920, podcast audio, February 22, 2017, https://www.mixcloud.com/TheJoeRoganExperience/920-gavin-mcinnes/.

offhanded manner, *Imperium* informs readers what will have transpired by 2000 or 2050, and the author often takes up the perspective of a man looking backward at 1948 from the twenty-first century, a time when Yockey's destiny-thinking will have become the dominant ideology.[127] This is not simply a utopian conceit: Yockey takes it for granted that the future will play out according to the cycles he has established in *Imperium*. His confidence in his powers of prediction is only outmatched by Spencer who, along with Edward Dutton, attempted to solve the Fermi Paradox by projecting the rise and fall of all extraterrestrial civilizations based on cyclical patterns laid out by race science.[128] The future is not speculative because in some sense it has already happened for fascists like Yockey.

Yockey's editor, Willis Carto, saw the science fictional potential contained within this philosophy. An immensely influential figure for postwar racists, Carto established the Liberty Lobby, a white nationalist political advocacy group, and went on to become a key organizer for Holocaust denialists and right-wing populists.[129] One of Carto's signal achievements came in 1968 when he helped transform a youth organization for George Wallace's presidential campaign into the National Youth Alliance, an antisemitic activist group that took Yockey's *Imperium* as its philosophical basis.[130] Carto succeeded in spreading Yockeyism throughout the far right.

Writing his introduction to *Imperium* at the height of public enthusiasm for the space race in 1962, Carto argues that "Western

127. Yockey, *Imperium*, 27–28.

128. Richard Spencer and Edward Dutton, "Where Are They?" *Radix*, podcast audio, April 10, 2021, author's archive. See also Matthew Andrew Sarraf, Michael Anthony Woodly of Menie, and Colin Feltham, *Modernity and Cultural Decline: A Biocultural Perspective* (Amherst, Mass.: Palgrave Macmillan, 2019), 19.

129. Leonard Zeskind, *Blood and Politics: The History of the White Nationalist Movement from the Margins to the Mainstream* (New York: Farrar, Straus and Giroux, 2009), 3–16.

130. Coogan, *Dreamer of the Day*, 518–19.

man is bound to conquer Space or to die in the attempt."[131] Carto
claims that colonial expansion constitutes "suicide" for white west-
erners because it inevitably leads to race mixing with subjugated
populations.[132] But now that "the White Man has burst the ties to
Earth," he is "headed for the stars" where he can fulfill his desire
to conquer a new "Frontier" without the risk of racial impurity.[133]
Citing Spengler's *Man and Technics,* Carto fantasizes about all the
seemingly impossible cosmic feats white men might dare to accomplish, such as rearranging the solar system, pushing back the
oceans, prolonging the sun's lifespan, and "[upgrading] the human
species through deliberate biological mechanics."[134] He claims that
none of this will happen, though, if white men do not stop humanity's degeneration. Jews are undermining Western civilization, he
insinuates, and soon "only barred doors [will keep] the jungle out
of the laboratory and the boudoir."[135] Carto fears that his white
astronauts will return to a Black planet.

Carto taps into a long tradition of thinking Western imperialism
and space exploration together. As John Rieder has shown, early science fiction emerged out of European anxieties and fantasies about
colonial encounters.[136] One can find presentiments of Carto's space
dream in stories that draw upon mythical accounts of New World
conquest to depict other planets as virgin territories waiting to be
tamed and exploited by white astronauts.[137] John De Witt Kilgore
observes that midcentury science fiction and popular science also
borrowed images of the U.S. western frontier from pulp fiction to

131. Willis Carto, "Introduction," to Francis Parker Yockey (Ulick
Varange), *Imperium: The Philosophy of History and Politics* (1948; repr.
Sausalito, Calif.: The Noontide Press, 1962), xxxviii–xl.

132. Carto, xl.

133. Carto, xl.

134. Carto, xl–xli.

135. Carto, xli.

136. John Rieder, *Colonialism and the Emergence of Science Fiction*
(Middletown, Conn.: Wesleyan University Press, 2008), 2–7.

137. Rieder, 30.

depict humankind's exploits in space.[138] Like nineteenth-century thinkers who believed that the frontier would resolve internal social conflicts back home, many authors suggested that shared conflicts with space aliens and other interstellar obstacles would heal earthly racial divisions.[139] For Carto, though, space is so appealing precisely because it is an empty void, one that allows for territorial expansion without any confrontations with otherness. Space solves racial conflict for Carto by being exclusively white.

The fascist's plans for interstellar colonization are obviously bound up in the history of European settler colonialism. As Menominee scholar Rowland Keshena Robinson suggests, the alt-right's "thirst for a *new frontier*, for *recolonization*, for territories, for a *white homeland*" constitutes a "thirst for the fulfilment of the settler dream."[140] Whiteness has always been predicated on the presumed right to invade, colonize, and possess space even if it is already held by Indigenous peoples.[141] White nationalist narratives reactivate the moment of colonization as a way of returning to what Alex Trimble Young would call "constituent power," a sovereign violence that makes as well as breaks laws.[142] In the myth of Wild West liberty, the power wielded by heavily armed white frontiersmen represented the pure potential to create a new world, one

138. Kilgore, *Astrofuturism*, 1–2, 78–79.

139. Kilgore, 84–85, 101.

140. Rowland Keshena Robinson, "Fascism & Antifascism: A Decolonial Perspective," *The Spectral Archive*, February 11, 2017, https://onkwehonwerising.wordpress.com/2017/02/11/fascism-anti-fascism-a-decolonial-perspective/; emphasis in original. See also Devin Zane Shaw, *Philosophy of Antifascism: Punching Nazis and Fighting White Supremacy* (New York: Rowman & Littlefield, 2020), 11–15.

141. Aileen Moreton-Robinson, *The White Possessive: Property, Power, and Indigenous Sovereignty* (Minneapolis: University of Minnesota Press, 2015), 49–50. See also Ruth Frankenberg, *White Women, Race Matters: The Social Construction of Whiteness* (Minneapolis: University of Minnesota Press, 1993), 15–17.

142. Alex Trimble Young, "The Settler Unchained: Constituent Power and Settler Violence," *Social Text* 33, no. 3 (124) (September 2015): 7–10.

opposed to the ossified actuality of constituted power prevailing back in the civilized states. These notions are often expressed in right-wing survivalist novels, "where the lawmaking violence of the frontier is unapologetically projected into the future as fantasy."[143] But they also appear in fascist space opera: white nationalist space colonization seeks to recreate this lawlessness on an even larger scale. The solar system becomes an unsettled place that allows for the free and creative exercise of white sovereignty—made possible by genocide.

The Turner Diaries

Fascists still dream of spaceflight. Popular culture has often wondered what would have happened if German rocket scientists such as Wernher von Braun had completed their research under Nazi auspices. id Software's revived *Wolfenstein* series, for example, gives players the chance to blast stormtroopers on the Moon and Venus in an alternate universe where the Fourth Reich won World War II. White nationalists, in turn, have responded to these narratives with their own retrofuturist fascist kitsch. We see this in fashwave, a flash-in-the-pan microtrend in online music that combined synthwave and vaporwave stylings with white nationalist themes. One fan described the wordless synthesizer noodlings on "Galactic Lebensraum" by CybernΔzi as "the sound of driving a futuristic, glistening sportscar (top down), through a twinkling neon cityscape, to a space port, to catch a light ship heading to [a whites-only] off-world resort, with your children and the woman you love."[144] The

---

143. Alex Trimble Young, "The Necropolitics of Liberty: Sovereignty, Fantasy, and United States Gun Culture," *Gun Culture* 9, no. 1 (Spring 2020), https://csalateral.org/forum/gun-culture/necropolitics-of-liberty-sovereignty-fantasy-us-gun-culture-young/.

144. Michael Hann, "'Fashwave': Synth Music Co-opted by the Far Right," *The Guardian*, December 14, 2016, https://www.theguardian.com/music/musicblog/2016/dec/14/fashwave-synth-music-co-opted-by-the-far-right.

album artwork combines a fascist Sonnenrad symbol and a *Tron*-looking grid with a pixelated image of Adolf Hitler in a mech suit taken from a boss fight in the 1992 game *Wolfenstein 3D*. Fashwave seems to have disappeared, but its glitchy neon aesthetic persists in some Nazi memes.

More important figures on the far right also shared Carto's vision. Carto's ideological rival, William Luther Pierce, spoke breathlessly of the Faustian spirit. Carto led the reformist faction dedicated to promoting white supremacy through electoral means, while Pierce rose to become the dominant figure of revolutionary white nationalism.[145] Amidst bitter conflict with Carto in the 1970s, Pierce captured the National Youth Alliance and founded its successor organization the National Alliance, a vanguard party for an entire generation of white power activists.[146] Although Pierce said that he never read Yockey's *Imperium,* we can clearly see resonances with his thought.[147]

In his writings on the Faust legend, Pierce argues that white men inherited the "basic restlessness" of the Faustian impulse, an inner voice that commands them to discover and master all things not out of Jewish acquisitiveness but out of a need to strive "for a new level of existence, for a fuller development of latent powers."[148] Pierce claims that the Faustian soul that animated European explorers and scientists also moved through him, encouraging him to become a science fiction fan and, in the early 1960s, to embark on a career in Caltech's Jet Propulsion Laboratory, which developed technology for NASA's space missions. Pierce was always fascinated by cosmic exploration: he maintained a lifelong interest in Nazi

---

145. Zeskind, *Blood and Politics,* 17–26.

146. Zeskind, 20–26.

147. Martin Durham, "From Imperium to Internet: The National Alliance and the American Extreme Right," *Patterns of Prejudice* 36, no. 3 (2002): 53.

148. William L. Pierce, "The Faustian Spirit," *National Vanguard,* April 12, 2015 [1978], https://web.archive.org/web/20220706122001/https://nationalvanguard.org/2015/04/the-faustian-spirit/.

rocket scientist Hermann Oberth, and he tried to join the U.S. Air Force with the hopes of becoming an astronaut someday but was rejected due to his excessive height and poor vision.[149] Reflecting on his discovery of science fiction at a young age, Pierce suggests that "our climb upward toward the stars" is driven by a Faustian spirit that makes white society "virile and forward-looking and willing to take chances."[150]

Although Pierce moved away from science fiction fandom and abandoned his career as a physicist, his best-known work is a serialized science fiction novel, *The Turner Diaries* (1978), a near-future dystopia that he wrote under the pseudonym "Andrew Macdonald." The novel's influence on white nationalism cannot be overstated: a movement Bible, *The Turner Diaries* inspired more than two hundred murders and forty terrorist attacks, including the 1995 Oklahoma City bombing.[151] Pierce frames the novel as a found document, the diaries from 1991 to 1993 of a white nationalist terrorist named Earl Turner, published more than a century in the future in commemoration of a global fascist revolution that ended in the genocide of all nonwhite people.

As Dan Sinykin points out, Pierce's apocalyptic novel "divorces humans from agency, delivering them to a larger inexorable force."[152] Racial egalitarian society will inevitably collapse due to unstoppable biological tendencies, *The Turner Diaries* suggest, but action can accelerate the process so that it falls before extinguishing the white

149. Robert S. Griffin, *The Fame of a Dead Man's Deeds: An Up-Close Portrait of White Nationalist William Pierce* (Bloomington, Ind.: 1st Books Library, 2001), 34.

150. William L. Pierce, "The Faustian Spirit and Political Correctness," *National Vanguard*, December 6, 2015 [July 29, 2000], https://web.archive .org/web/20240317004616/https://nationalvanguard.org/2015/12/the -faustian-spirit-and-political-correctness/.

151. J. M. Berger, "The Turner Legacy: The Storied Origins and Enduring Impact of White Nationalism's Deadly Bible," *The International Centre for Counter-Terrorism—The Hague (ICCT) Evolutions in Counter-Terrorism*, 1 (2016): 22.

152. Sinykin, *Neoliberal Apocalypse*, 58.

race. In the white supremacist risk regime, white people appear as risk-takers whose dangerous enterprises might usher in a better world, but nonwhite people appear as risks whose foreseeable threat must be preempted through violence.[153] The novel attempts to resolve this binary through bloodshed: white nationalists such as Turner are willing to forfeit their lives if it means killing nonwhite people. Pierce's legacy has therefore been stochastic terrorism, with the all-too-predictable suffering and death that follows.

Turner is somewhat of a tech geek, spending much of the novel inventing distributed communication networks for the movement's terror cells before finally destroying the Jewish conspiracy's central computer in a suicide attack. It's fitting, then, that the novel describes his initiation into white nationalism in science fictional terms. Time seems to stop after he is given a binder known as the Book that provides a full explication of the movement's real beliefs. He looks up to realize that hours have passed while he remained completely absorbed in the manuscript's message: "It was as if I had just returned to earth—to the room—after a thousand-year voyage through space."[154] The book seems to take him "out of this world" to a vantage point where he can see not only the entire planet's nations and races but also all of earth's history, including "the unlimited possibilities which the centuries and the millennia ahead hold for us."[155]

What he finds in the Book is remarkably similar to the opening chapter of Yockey's *Imperium*, which begins by taking the reader up to "the astral regions" where we "can glance toward this spinning earth-ball."[156] Floating in "exterior darkness where no breath stirs," the reader observes the continents and "population-streams," noticing that on the European peninsula "the greatest intensity of

153. Katharyne Mitchell, "Pre-Black Futures," *Antipode* 41, no. S1 (2009), 239–61.

154. Macdonald, *Turner Diaries*, 71.

155. Macdonald, 33.

156. Yockey, *Imperium*, 3.

movement exists."[157] Yockey switches to a spiritual or, perhaps, four-dimensional perspective that allows his audience to see future potential in the form of a "light stream" that today flows exclusively from Europeans and their descendants.[158] From there, Yockey transports the reader through the ages—"out here we have the freedom of time as well as the freedom of space"—speeding through generations to watch civilizations rise and decline before finally returning the reader to earth where they are asked to intervene to stop the impending fall of Western civilization.[159]

As in Turner's conversion experience, Yockey suggests that race consciousness allows white men to transcend the limits of space-time and adopt a God's-eye perspective that will provide the knowledge needed to resolve the present crisis. Turner's triumph appears not as a great risk but as a foregone conclusion. From the book's foreword, we already know that he has succeeded and, regardless of his fate, the white nationalists will have obtained power by 2099. The found-manuscript structure of the book confers upon the reader the same omniscience as Turner when he reads the white nationalist's sacred text. Try as it might to evoke a feeling of suspense, Pierce's novel leaves nothing to chance.

The Fascist Simulacrum

White nationalist discourses on the future seem to take place in the future perfect, describing what will have happened once the Aryan ethnostate or imperium has ascended to power. This is the tense used to narrate Lacan's mirror stage, which some critics read as a theory of fascism.[160] Whiteness is therefore a speculative fiction:

157. Yockey, 3.
158. Yockey, 3.
159. Yockey, 4.
160. Jane Gallop, *Reading Lacan* (Ithaca: Cornell University Press, 1985), 81–83; Hal Foster, "Armor Fou," *October* 56 (Spring 1991): 64–97; Susan Buck-Morss, "Aesthetics and Anaesthetics: Walter Benjamin's Artwork Essay Reconsidered," *October* 62 (Autumn 1992): 3–41.

it relies on an anticipatory fantasy that white men have the power to someday achieve the impossible goal of perfect mastery over themselves and others. The Faustian spirit locks itself into an irresolvable contradiction: its powers of open-ended transcendence and unpredictable risk-taking rely on the assured arrival of the endpoint that will retroactively confirm these abilities. The alt-right proclaims the negation of the here-and-now, but then it betrays itself by committing to a future whose sole purpose is to monumentalize their present identities as glorious, necessary, and eternal. They say they want tomorrow to reveal that they have infinite potential to be anything and everything, but they really want a future that merely confirms who they are as fixed and inevitable.

Faustian science fiction therefore turns out to be bad science fiction. Science fiction at its best is a radically historicizing genre that reveals the present as contingent while allowing us to imagine how things might be otherwise.[161] White nationalists, however, are profoundly antihistorical. Whereas strong science fiction asks us to confront the possibility of a fundamental break with the existent, Faustian science fiction consoles its fascist fans by positing the essential continuity of blood and time. Speculative whiteness therefore represents the kind of pseudo-rupture that Alain Badiou described in his diagnosis of Nazism's radical evil as a "simulacrum" of the event.[162]

Beyond serving as a method for achieving historical consciousness, science fiction has also been understood as an opportunity to think through racial, cultural, and other differences.[163] Aliens often appear as metaphors for the other, but extraterrestrials are strangely absent from most alt-right engagements with science fiction.

161. Carl Freedman, *Critical Theory and Science Fiction* (Middletown, Conn.: Wesleyan University Press, 2000), 54–55.

162. Alain Badiou, *Ethics: An Essay on the Understanding of Evil*, trans. Peter Hallward (New York: Verso, 2001), 72–77.

163. Isiah Lavender III, *Race in American Science Fiction* (Bloomington: Indiana University Press, 2011), 8.

Spencer makes clear that he considers communication with human as well as nonhuman others to be impossible when he quotes a scientist from Andrei Tarkovsky's *Solaris* (1972): "I must tell you that we really have no desire to conquer any cosmos. We want to extend the earth up to its borders. We don't know what to do with other worlds. We don't need other worlds: we need a mirror."[164] Spencer tendentiously interprets him as speaking on behalf of white civilization to say, "We can't know anything beyond our own history and tradition."[165] White people may explore the stars, Spencer argues, but they can never make contact with others because they'll always "project" their desires onto them.[166] Speculative whiteness will always remain self-imprisoned in a racist solipsism that prevents it from imagining anything outside or after itself. Once more, the alt-right promises a bold new future in space but it never achieves escape velocity from white supremacy's perpetual present.

164. Richard Spencer, Colin Lidell, and Andy Nowicki, "Man & Superman," *Vanguard Radio*, podcast audio, April 15, 2013, https://archive .org/details/ManSuperman_201905.

165. Spencer, Lidell, and Nowicki.

166. Spencer, Lidell, and Nowicki.

Conclusion: Tomorrow Belongs to Everyone

SCIENCE FICTION CULTURE SWIFTLY MOBILIZED against the far right in the wake of the Trump election. Readers showed renewed interest in fascist dystopias and alternative histories by Sinclair Lewis, Katharine Burdekin, Philip K. Dick, Octavia Butler, and Philip Roth. Women protesters wore habits modeled on the ones featured in the Hulu adaptation of Margaret Atwood's *The Handmaid's Tale*. A wave of antifascist speculative narratives appeared in response to the fascist resurgence. N. K. Jemisin figured white supremacy as an extradimensional invasion in *The City We Became* (2020), and P. Djèlí Clark's *Ring Shout* (2020) imagined a supernatural battle against demonic Klansmen. Superhero narratives—a genre with deep connections to vigilante violence—grappled with right-wing extremism through television adaptations such as *Watchmen* (2019) and *The Boys* (2019–).

Gene Luen Yang and Gurihiru's *Superman Smashes the Klan* (2019–20) directly addresses the temporal dimensions of white supremacy. The graphic novel remediates the 1946 *Superman* radio serial "Clan of the Fiery Cross," a highly successful narrative that mocked actual Ku Klux Klan codewords and rituals to discredit the organization.[1] The Man of Tomorrow, himself an immigrant,

1. Gene Luen Yang, "Superman and Me," in *Superman Smashes the Klan* by Gene Luen Yang and Gurihiru, (Burbank, Calif.: DC, 2020), 236–37.

fights a robed white supremacist who has been terrorizing the Lees, a Chinese American family. When the Grand Scorpion sneers at him, "The Lees aren't 'your own!' You share no blood with them! No history!" Superman responds, "We are bound together by the future. We all share the same tomorrow."[2] When white nationalism tried to enroll science fiction into its metapolitical project, the genre fought back.

Other science fiction creators framed the struggle against fascism as a fight for the future. Annalee Newitz's *The Future of Another Timeline* (2019) features a war between feminist time travelers and a group of male supremacist incels who want to prevent all future timeline edits and freeze in place a future dystopia where women are nothing more than genetically engineered procreative vessels, "making it illegal for people to have agency over their futures. Over the future of the species, even."[3] Silvia Moreno-Garcia takes up similar concerns in *Mexican Gothic* (2020), which features a white supremacist patriarch who uses a pale fungus to achieve immortality by imprinting his mind onto a new host body every generation. The villain of the novel—an English settler-colonist in Mexico— exploits others' bodies to project his identity into the future. After destroying him along with his monstrous family home, the novel's mixed-race protagonist rejects the idea that history should be a "cursed circle," an ouroboros of whiteness, and chooses instead to affirm that "the future . . . could not be predicted, and the shape of things could not be divined."[4]

But perhaps the most formally sophisticated rebuttal to fascists comes in the unlikely form of Chuck Tingle's queer absurdist science fiction erotica. Tingle has often parodied the far right: he creat-

---

2. Emphasis removed. Gene Luen Yang and Gurihiru, *Superman Smashes the Klan* (Burbank, Calif.: DC, 2020), 220–21.

3. Annalee Newitz, *The Future of Another Timeline* (New York: Tor, 2019), 261.

4. Silvia Moreno-Garcia, *Mexican Gothic* (2020; repr. New York: Del Rey, 2021), 301.

ed a fake version of Breitbart.com that included the "Top 5 Alt-Right Basements," and after Trump was elected he went on a mission to reverse this "timeline mistake."[5] When Theodore Beale—blogging as Vox Day—attempted to embarrass the Hugo Awards by nominating Tingle's *Space Raptor Butt Invasion* (2015), Tingle responded by trolling Beale with a website that satirized the Rabid Puppies and drove traffic to support projects created by Beale's past targets, N. K. Jemisin, Zoë Quinn, and Rachel Swirsky.[6] Tingle's *Slammed in the Butt by My Hugo Nomination* (2016) goes further to undermine fascist temporality by imagining a multiverse filled with parallel worlds in which the most fundamental ontological level is composed of queer utopian desire. Entire universes change retroactively in mid-sentence to fulfill the author's yearning for infinitely diverse bodies in infinite combinations. Tingle represents the most uncompromising antidote to the fixed identitarian future, but all antifascist science fiction presents history as what we make of it. Tomorrow belongs to everyone.

Although this book examines the recent past, it must be understood as a historical study. The alt-right collapsed in the aftermath of Charlottesville. Many of its members left the alt-right for more backward-looking far-right groups that see themselves as faithful to fundamentalist religious traditions or the memory of totalitarian regimes such as Nazi Germany. At the same time, a number of fascists abandoned the metapolitical project of changing the culture and instead encouraged their comrades to take up the gun in mass shootings such as the Christchurch mosque attacks. Even Richard Spencer, who conducted an online class on science fiction cinema in

5. Chuck Tingle qtd in Andrew Ferguson, "The President as a Shrieking Pile of Void Crabs; or, The Cosmically Horrific Satire of Dr. Chuck Tingle," *Academia.edu*, January 5, 2018, https://www.academia.edu/35591273/The_President_as_a_Shrieking_Pile_of_Void_Crabs.

6. Aja Romano, "Satirical Erotica Author Chuck Tingle's Massive Troll of Conservative Sci-Fi Fans, explained," *Vox*, May 26, 2016, https://www.vox.com/2016/5/26/11759842/chuck-tingle-hugo-award-rabid-puppies-explained.

2022, seems to have lost his optimistic belief in the Faustian impulse. He still podcasts about speculative narratives, but his interpretations increasingly obsess over paranoid antisemitic readings that reduce futuristic media to echoes of ancient mythologies supposedly invented by the Jews to corrupt white gentiles. Nevertheless, speculative whiteness—the idea that white men are the future—continues to be a pervasive idea in many far-right circles.

Even if the alt-right may have waned, we shouldn't be complacent about fascism. As one commentator has suggested, this has been a creative if uneven period for fascist activists who have followed every political failure with new "speculative attempts" to invent formations that'll allow them to succeed in "the mainstreaming of a violent, extra-parliamentary right."[7] As we have seen, the fascists claim they'll unleash new potentials, but if they succeed it'll only mean the strangulation of all possibilities for an emancipatory future. Therefore, if we want to maintain our hope for a future that belongs to everyone, we must dismantle the limits imposed upon our utopian imaginations by speculative whiteness.

7. Richard Seymour, "Is It Fascism If It's Still Incompetent?" *Patreon*, January 6, 2021, https://www.patreon.com/posts/is-it-still-if-45896691.

Acknowledgments

Thanks to everyone who helped me along the way, including andré m. carrington, Ben Allen, Anindita Banerjee, Ranjodh Singh Dhaliwal, Camestros Felapton, Harrison Fluss, Elizabeth Freeman, David Higgins, Caroline Hovanec, Mark Jerng, Sarah Juliet Lauro, Colin Milburn, Steven Mollmann, Benjamin Noys, Benjamin O'Dell, Joshua Pearson, Jon Phillips, Brett Rogers, Elda María Román, Elizabeth Sandifer, Stephen Schryer, Alexandra Minna Stern, Sherryl Vint, and my family. I have appreciated the editorial assistance of Leah Pennywark, Mike Stoffel, and everyone else at the University of Minnesota Press's Forerunners series. I began thinking about this book while working at the ModLab at the University of California, Davis, and the *Los Angeles Review of Books* gave me my first opportunity to write about fascism and science fiction. The introduction and chapter 2 include revised material first presented in a different form in the Los Angeles Review of Books in "Race Consciousness: Fascism and Frank Herbert's 'Dune'" on November 19, 2020. Finally, I would like to thank all the university and public libraries that have provided invaluable assistance in this project, including the Peter J. Shields Library at the University of California, Davis, the Macdonald–Kelce Library at the University of Tampa, the Collins Memorial Library at the University of Puget Sound, and the Stephen O. Murray and Keelung Hong Special Collections at Michigan State University Libraries.

(Continued from page iii)

Forerunners: Ideas First

Jordan S. Carroll is the author of *Reading the Obscene: Transgressive Editors and the Class Politics of US Literature*. He received his PhD in English literature from the University of California, Davis.